Mermaids, Mummies, and Mastodons ☞

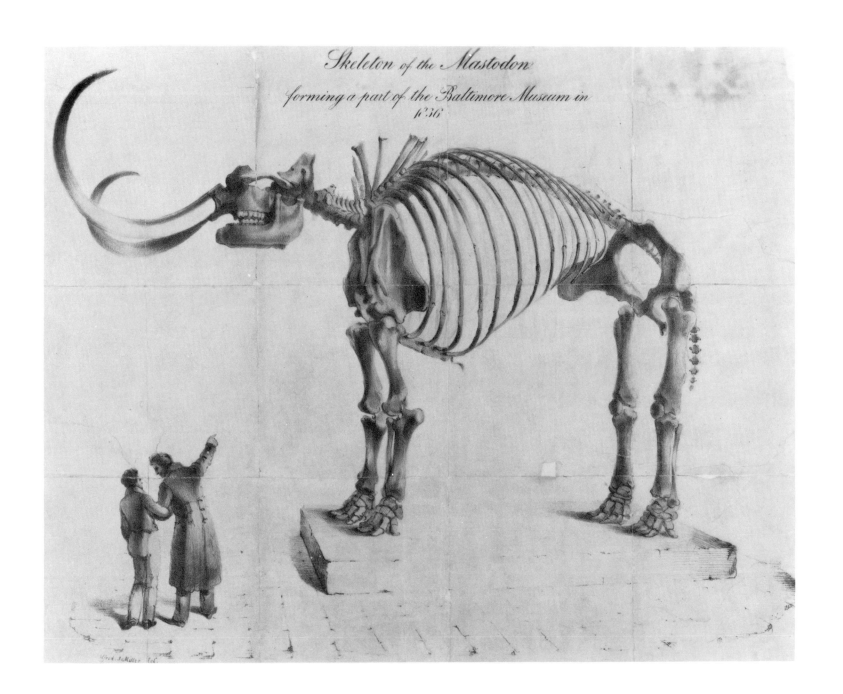

Skeleton of the Mastodon
forming a part of the Baltimore Museum in
1836

Mermaids, Mummies, and Mastodons:
The Emergence of the American Museum

 Published by the

American Association of Museums

Washington, D.C.

Edited by William T. Alderson

for the Baltimore City Life Museums

Baltimore, Md.

1992

American
Association
of Museums

Published by the American Association of Museums, 1225 Eye St. NW, Suite 200, Washington, D.C., 20005. ©1992. All rights reserved. No portion of this book may be reproduced in any form for any purpose without prior written permission from the publisher.

Coordinating editor in charge: John Strand
Production editor: Amy Grissom
Associate coordinating editor: Susannah Cassedy
Designer: Polly Sexton, Washington, D.C.
Printer: Collins Lithographing Inc., Baltimore, MD.

Library of Congress Cataloging-in-Publication Data
Mermaids, mummies, and mastodons : the emergence of the American museum.
    p.   cm.
    Includes bibliographical references and index.
    ISBN 0-931201-15-2
    1. Museums—United States—History. 2. Peale family 3. Barnum, P.T. (Phineas Taylor), 1810–1891. I. American Association of Museums. II. Baltimore City Life Museums.
    AM11.M56   1992
069' .0973—dc20   92-29830
                                                                CIP

Cover:
The Exhumation of the Mastodon (detail)
   By Charles Willson Peale, 1806-08
   Baltimore City Life Museums

Frontispiece:
Skeleton of the Mastodon
   Lithograph by Alfred Jacob Miller
   reproduced in A Brief Description of the Skeleton . . . in the Baltimore Museum *(Baltimore, 1836)*
   Baltimore City Life Museums

❀ Contents

A ⋆
Museum
and Gallery of the Fine Arts in Holliday Street
Established by Rembrandt Peale AD 1813 Cost 18,000 D.ˢ

R.C.Long Archᵗ

CITY OF BALTIMORE, 1830
A view from Federal Hill across the Basin

 *Foreword*

Nancy Brennan

 *Baltimore From Federal Hill* (left)
Aquatint by William J. Bennett, 1831
Maryland Historical Society

Both Rembrandt and Rubens Peale witnessed the growth of the nation's third largest city. By 1830 Baltimore could boast of impressive churches, monuments, and commercial buildings, and 80,000 inhabitants, most of whom lived within a mile of the waterfront.

Charles Willson Peale's well-known self-portrait, "The Artist in His Museum," (page 78) is the central image and the unifying metaphor for the project, *"Mermaids, Mummies, and Mastodons"* in each of its three component parts—the exhibition, public programs, and this book. Like the mature Peale who lifts the velvet curtain to invite the viewer to discover the wonders of both the holdings of his Philadelphia museum and the museum setting itself, the project team worked to reveal the story of America's oldest museum building, the 1814 Peale Museum in Baltimore, and through its interpretation, to reflect on our nation's earliest museum efforts. Along the way we were captivated by the museum profession's colorful origins, a melange of visionary leadership, intellectual excitement, self-interest and competition, market instincts and entrepreneurship, and daily frustrations of sustaining a viable enterprise.

The graceful, human-scale Peale Museum is the institutional foundation of the Baltimore City Life Museums, a system of seven sites devoted to the research and interpretation of urban history for a broad public audience. The Peale Museum is also the key object in *Mermaids, Mummies, and Mastodons*. As we approached the close of its second century, we wanted to understand the decisions and struggles Rembrandt and Rubens Peale faced in the 15 years they successively operated the ambitious enterprise formally titled "Museum

and Gallery of Fine Arts," and to set these men in the greater context of the contributions made by their father and other American museum pioneers.

The Peale Museum is also a symbol of the contest between varying visions of the American museum as a civic institution. The visions of Rembrandt and Charles Willson Peale were significantly at odds with each other, as authors Ruth Helms and John W. Durel point out. The elder Peale's proposition that the value of museums as an instrument of scientific study and public education was such that they merited public support was discouraged at every turn. Meanwhile, his son Rembrandt recast his father's dream in a different mold. Rembrandt established his museum as a profitmaking commercial enterprise catering to a paying audience with a blend of galleries displaying paintings and portraits, natural and ethnographic specimens, and technological curiosities, with a fashionable salon of genteel entertainments. Perhaps we can take some comfort in this clash of visions: Today's tension between the mission of museums as a social instrument deserving public funding and the common expectation that museums must run like businesses on financial planning and operating structures which mimic commercial business models has been with us since the birth of the American museum.

If funding was a preoccupation, it was nevertheless secondary to the central adventure of amassing and presenting objects of wonder and curiosity to a public hungry to see the products of this period of learning, travel, and exploration. This story of discovery, research, and dispersion of knowledge, whether through vehicles as diverse as libraries, amateur academies, museums, or itinerant showmen, was the core of the Peale Museum's featured exhibition, "Mermaids, Mummies, and Mastodons: the Evolution of the American Museum," chiefly curated by Richard Flint. Over four years in the making and funded in large part by the National Endowment for the Humanities, the exhibit resulted in ground-breaking research and the exciting assembly of little-known early 19th-century objects, thanks to the generous cooperation of over forty lenders.

Mr. Flint was assisted by many talented and dedicated professionals, both on and off the City Life Museums' staff. While it is dangerous to note just a few among many who deserve our thanks, Assistant Director John Durel, Curator of Local History Dean Krimmel, then-Registrar Jane Woltereck, Carol McCurdy, Mary Markey, James Dickson, and Otto Gast contributed directly to the high professional standards evident in the final product. Special mention should go also to Beth Miles of the design firm of Miles Fridberg Molinaroli, whose talent and design vision in the development of this show were matched by her dedication to a good client-consultant process.

Finally, the curatorial team wishes to thank conservation consultant Catherine Hawks, whose professional guidance helped to maintain the well-being of the numerous loaned objects. We are delighted that the creativity and hard work of Mr. Flint and the rest of the project team were honored with an award in the 1990 American Association of Museums Curators' Committee Exhibit Competition.

Public programs enhanced the exhibit by bringing to the Peale Museum scholars and re-enactors to describe, interpret, and recreate "rational amusements" once offered by the Peales and other early museum operators. Funded by the W. K. Kellogg Foundation and organized by Education Specialist Eileen Langholtz, these programs ranged from an exhibition of sword-swallowing to lectures on geology and Egyptology and helped our public to understand the extra dimension of entertainment that enlivened Rembrandt's and Rubens's museum.

This book is the enduring legacy of the entire project, and it has been executed skillfully by Assistant Director John Durel, with liberal doses of enthusiasm and good ideas from John Strand, director of publications of the American Association of Museums. We are delighted to be publishing this book with AAM, and thank Executive Director Edward H. Able, Jr. for his sponsorship of this venture. Moreover, this book would not have been possible without the financial support of the National Endowment for the Humanities and the W. K. Kellogg Foundation. In addition, we gratefully acknowledge the intellectual support of Marsha Semmel and Frederic Miller of NEH and Joel J. Orosz of the Kellogg Foundation.

To aid us as editor, we could not have been more fortunate in having the assistance of William T. Alderson, whose career includes serving as director of the Museum Studies Program at the University of Delaware and currently as member of the graduate faculty of Wake Forest University, where he teaches the management of cultural institutions. At the same time we are privileged to have two major influences in the museum field join us as authors: Gary Kulik, assistant director for academic programs at the National Museum of American History, and Edward P. Alexander, whose long career has been devoted to creating the modern museum profession.

In offering this volume of essays, we invite you to step back in time before the emergence of the complex institution we know as today's American museum. Assume the role of an early museum operator in a society with few tenable role models, including museums. Where would you start? Where are you headed? ❀ ❀ ❀

Introduction

Gary Kulik

The Exhumation of the Mastodon (left, detail)
By Charles Willson Peale, 1806–08
Baltimore City Life Museums

In this family scene, Charles Willson Peale shows us some of America's earliest museum operators: Peale himself is on the left; his son Rembrandt is in the center, holding the drawing of the mastodon bones; and son Rubens, with a hat on, stands behind two younger members of the family.

Charles Willson Peale and his family continue to attract attention. He and they have been the subject of several recent books, essays, dissertations, and exhibitions. The Peale papers continue to be published. The Peale name graces one museum. What accounts for our interest in them, and especially in Charles Willson Peale? Surely we are attracted by the breadth of his interests. He was an artist, scientist, museum founder. It is that very breadth that makes him so unlike us, however, and closer to the Renaissance than to the twentieth century. Why does he continue to compel the attention of historians, art historians, and museum professionals?[1] For museum professionals, in particular, Peale seems to have faced peculiarly modern dilemmas. His long struggle for financial support, his efforts to create a museum that was both entertaining and scholarly, and his attempts to use it self-consciously as an instrument of democracy, compel him to us. His problems seem not unlike ours. It is easy to see him as a precurser, easy to locate him, as he has been located, as part of our usable past.

Recently, Michael Shapiro, in an essay "The Public and the Museum," in his edited *The Museum: A Reference Guide,* described the traditional story of the museum's rise as a "four-act moral drama" beginning in the mid-sixteenth century and continuing to the present, a drama in which aristocratic patronage and the fear of vulgar crowds gives way in stages as visionary and public spirited museum workers and their allies capture museums, successfully argue for public funding, and throw open the doors, like Andrew Jackson at the White House, to a grateful but surprisingly well disciplined populace. This is a morality play that continues to play well. Peale has a key place in such a tale, somewhere in Act 2, "The Enlightenment," as the first American visionary. But Shapiro offered his interpretation as a critique. For him and for others, the traditional view obscured both the past and the present, leading museum professionals to feel entirely too self-satisfied about themselves and in the process distorting the past to fit the needs of the present.[2]

In this light, Peale has been seen as a pioneer who first faced problems—of funding, of audience, of presentation—that current museum professionals have come increasingly close to solving. He, of course, never solved those problems. This is a view that reduces him to the status of a quaint father figure of no real relevance to the present, a figure important only to the pre-history of the modern museum movement. He deserves better.

Let us look at three issues that Peale faced and that we continue to face, attentive to both the differences that separate Peale from us and the unresolved nature of those problems. First is the problem of funding. Who funds us and what do we owe to those who do? Second is the problem of audience. Who comes to see

Charles Willson Peale gave this painting to his son Rubens, and it probably hung in the Baltimore Museum from 1822, when Rubens became manager, until 1825, when he moved to New York to open a museum there.

us and why does that matter? Third, how do we balance our commitment to research and scholarship with our efforts to entertain and educate?

Peale's long effort to secure federal or state funding for his museum ultimately failed. Ruth Helm's essay in this collection elaborates that case. In the absence of government funding, early nineteenth-century museums were forced to rely either on gate receipts or on philanthropy. John Durel's account of Rubens Peale's efforts to attract customers, and his reprinting of the time line from the Peale Museum's exhibition "Mermaids, Mummies, and Mastodons" suggests how difficult it was to attract paying visitors. In their effort to do so, some museums came to embrace a crass commercialism, the logical extension of which was P. T. Barnum. On the other side, private museums and historical societies founded by philanthropic elites tended increasingly to withdraw from public education. No one in the mid-nineteenth century could have believably predicted that Peale's position was the one that would eventually win.

But win it did. Public support for museums, federal, state, and local, is now massive, and at least since the 1930s, and increasingly since the 1960s, has been strongly associated with democratization, an opening to new subjects and new audiences. It is very tempting to read this as the triumph of an enlightened citizenry, as public funding saving the museum from the perils of commerce and from conservative aesthetes with no interest in public education. It would be tempting, but not very helpful.

In the first place, Peale tried to make arguments for public support at a time when the

public just was not interested. The place of government in nineteenth-century life was far smaller and circumscribed than it would become. Few were prepared to defend the use of public monies to support culture.

This is an argument that has been made with increasing force in recent years, and can no longer be dismissed as the cranky ravings of conservatives. Not a single commentator on a recent "This Week with David Brinkley" could summon a single argument to defend the public funding of art.

Rather than seeing Peale as a lonely seer later vindicated, we may come to see him in more familiar terms, someone like ourselves struggling to advance an argument in the face of a skeptical public. Why should taxpayers fund us and what do we owe them? Peale's arguments, that intelligent collecting and preservation and interpretation would "humanize the minds, promote harmony, and aid Virtue," may sound odd, even archaic.[3] We can perhaps do better, and we may have to, especially now at a time when a national consensus supporting the public funding of the arts and humanities seems more fragile than it has been in years.

The recent criticism, however, may be salutary. We need to remind ourselves that there is a social compact, and that we do have obligations. The public monies that flow to us are not entitlements. Peale understood that better than most of us. There has been far too little public discussion of what museums owe the public.

Public monies have not freed us from the dangers of commercialism, nor the Barnumesque tendency to pander. Publicly supported cultural institutions have erred, in

recent years, in confusing their missions with those of their corporate donors. A small number of museums seem untroubled by the content of their teaching and more concerned at choosing popular exhibition topics.[4]

Contempt for the public has resurfaced, less among stodgy conservatives defending their collections from the "wretched public," as one British museum director once labelled his visitors, but oddly and most notably from some artists and their supporters. The claim that denial of funding equals censorship, or the Romantic claim that artists owe us only their creativity wherever that should lead, speaks to a deep failure of public vision, often accompanied by an elitism that might make even Matthew Arnold blush. In the midst of public hearings in the early 1980s on the fate of "Tilted Arc," Richard Serra's controversial New York City sculpture, one of Serra's defenders dismissed his critics by questioning their qualifications. None, he said, had an advanced degree in art.[5]

Who comes to see what we do and how has our audience changed over time? Shapiro's morality play suggests that we know the answer, and the answer is that we have gradually become more inclusive over time. We do not yet have sufficient evidence to be decisive, but there is reason to doubt the story.

Lawrence Levine, in *Highbrow/Lowbrow* has offered one challenge by arguing that the great distance that now separates elite and popular culture had its origins in the late nineteenth century, and that the great cultural institutions of that era, museums, concert halls, and theaters, played their part in creating a largely upper middle class audience for themselves. According to Levine, the ante-bellum period was more fluid, the lines between elite and popular culture not as firmly drawn. Ordinary Americans knew some Shakespeare, and attended concerts and plays. Did they attend museums too?[6]

David Brigham, in his paper for this volume, has new evidence that they did not. Despite Peale's democratic intent, his audience was largely an elite one, richer and better educated than Philadelphia's populace as a whole. Peale's audience looks little different than our own. Many contemporary audience surveys suggest that despite our efforts at inclusion, despite our own democratic intent, museum going remains the pastime of relatively affluent, relatively well-educated families. We appear then not to have solved the problem that Peale first faced. We have no reason to feel self-satisfied. The history of museum audiences then may not be a history of gradual inclusion, but a history of remarkable continuity in which museums have remained narrow and limited in their appeal. The problem is even crueler, given the increase in public support, drawn from a tax code far more regressive than it needs to be. Thus the tax dollars of the broad middle class have been used to subvent upper middle-class cultural activities. What is the proper balance between research and public education? Peale and his sons, with many fewer resources than today's museum directors, set an admirable model, balancing the need for both research and education. In her essay in this volume, Sally Gregory Kohlstedt suggests the depth of the Peales' commitment to both while making clear how difficult it was to succeed at both. The private natural history societies tended increasingly to concentrate on research to the

⚘ Rubens Peale
By Rembrandt Peale, 1834
Wadsworth Atheneum, Hartford. William B. and
Mary Arabella Goodwin Collection

Appearing prosperous in this portrait painted by his
brother shortly before the financial panic of 1837,
Rubens was active in operating the three Peale museums
in New York, Baltimore, and Philadelphia.

exclusion of public education, and the Smithsonian Institution's first secretary, Joseph Henry, argued that research and the increase of knowledge ought to be the new institution's first priority.[7] Few voices today would be so bold or so single-minded. The advocates of public education as the principal mission of museums have been victorious, and the public has been well served. Museums have been increasingly attentive to their audiences, in some cases revamping their publication programs to reach a larger public.

In properly serving the public, museums need to remember that the basis of education is research. This is especially true of museums of history, art, and science, the three fields in which the Peales established their significance. Museums have two choices. They can do research themselves, or they can turn to the work of university scholars and others. In actual practice, most museums do a bit of both, though nurturing museum research involves the existence of resources and of long-term commitments that typically only larger museums can afford. Even they have

been subjected to increasing pressure from directors intent on maximizing short-term goals. The mission statement of a major museum of anthropology makes it clear that the days of long-term, pure research are over. "Highly-directed, short-term, secondary research," it claimed, "will be the norm for several years to come." What the long-term costs of such an approach might be are left unstated. Yet surely there is a warning in the recent experience of a few American history museums where the long-term goals of research and conservation were sacrificed to the unsuccessful pursuit of larger audiences. We may be grateful, without surrendering to elitism, that those monks who carefully saved and transcribed ancient documents did not also have to run museums.[8]

In the end, Peale offers us not a model for what we ought to do, nor a hero for our time, nor a worthy precursor to our perfected present, but a figure, different from us, but significantly similar to continue to provoke our interest and our respect. Neither he nor we could ask for more. ❈ ❈ ❈

Mermaids, Mummies, and Mastodons ☞

❧ Mermaids, Mummies, and Mastodons: An Exhibition on the Evolution of Early American Museums

Edward P. Alexander

❧ *The Long Room* (left)
Watercolor drawing by Titian Ramsey Peale II, 1822
Detroit Institute of Arts, Founders Society purchase

This drawing is a faithful rendering of the largest room in the Philadelphia Peale Museum and accurately documents the museum's displays and arrangements. Charles Willson Peale used it as a guide for the background in his famous self-portrait (p. 78). It was also used as a basis for the recreated museum room in "Mermaids, Mummies, and Mastodons."

The exhibition, "Mermaids, Mummies, and Mastodons: The Evolution of the American Museum," which ran from December 1, 1990, to June 30, 1992, at the Peale Museum in Baltimore, sought to help the public understand the early roles played by museums in American life. In particular, it examined the work of the Peale family and of P.T. Barnum to illustrate the parallel and sometimes complementary roles of research and entertainment in the historical development of museums. It interpreted early museums as one of the means by which new knowledge reached a popular audience.

Based on research by Richard Flint, the exhibition curator, "Mermaids, Mummies, and Mastodons" brought together 190 objects from forty lenders. The centerpiece was a re-created museum room, inspired by Charles Willson Peale's self-portrait, "The Artist in his Museum," and by his son Titian's sketch of the Long Room in the Philadelphia Museum. The re-created room included reproduction chandeliers to simulate gas lighting, a reproduced fiberglass mastodon skeleton, mounted to imitate period mounting techniques, and exhibit cases modeled on those in the Peale

illustrations. Numerous natural history and ethnographic objects filled the cases, including the outer coffin of Padihershef, the first Egyptian mummy brought to America; objects from Africa, the Northwest American coast, and islands of the Pacific; butterflies mounted by Titian Peale for the Philadelphia Museum; and birds as exhibited by Charles Willson Peale. Above the cases hung portraits of public figures, military heroes, and scientists.

Tracking down the many objects once displayed by the Peales was a major undertaking. The Baltimore Museum was dispersed at auction in 1858, and the whereabouts of most of its objects is unknown. A few surviving mastodon bones are in the collections of the Baltimore City Life Museums. P.T. Barnum acquired the collections of the Peale museums in Philadelphia and New York, and merged them with his own American Museum, which burned. However, some of the Philadelphia collection was acquired jointly with Moses Kimball, operator of the Boston Museum. Ultimately Kimball's collection passed to two museums at Harvard University, the Peabody Museum and the Museum of Comparative Zoology. The mummy Padi-

Reproduction mastodon skeleton (left)
Baltimore City Life Museums
Photo by Bob Creamer

The centerpiece of the "Mermaids, Mummies, and Mastodons" exhibition was a fiberglass reproduction of the skeleton of a mastodon, similar to the skeletons displayed by Charles Willson Peale and Rembrandt Peale in Philadelphia and Baltimore, respectively. Suspending the skeleton by chains from the ceiling simulated the technique used in Baltimore.

hershef's tour of the east coast in 1824 included a stay at Peale's Baltimore Museum. The mummy belongs to the Massachusetts General Hospital; the coffin is in the collection of the George Walter Vincent Smith Art Museum, Springfield, Mass. Two Philadelphia institutions were also major lenders of Peale material: the Academy of Natural Sciences and the American Philosophical Society.

In other galleries, "Mermaids, Mummies, and Mastodons" covered early collecting efforts which influenced Charles Willson Peale, Peale's own expedition to excavate the mastodon skeletons, and the relationship between museums and other means of spreading knowledge. The final room featured a timeline of the Baltimore museum, and a performance stage inspired by the lecture gallery stage in Barnum's American Museum in New York City.

This exhibition showed clearly the democratic development of the American museum and its success in using objects to provide valuable instruction and yet be entertaining so as to attract a large audience. Its title, though dramatic and amusing, is somewhat misleading in that Barnum's Fiji mermaid, Peale's mastodon, and the traveling Egyptian mummy case of Padihershef shown at this museum in 1824 are not the essence of the exhibition. Instead, the numerous objects supplemented by printed materials and instructive labels illustrated the American museum's development, educational worth, and appeal to the general public.

Peale's Philadelphia Museum carried on by the artist and his sons from 1786 into the 1850s was the most important early American museum. The first of its two chief aims was to teach natural science and, to a lesser degree,

art and some history. He sought to arrange animals from the lowly worm to human beings according to the Linnaean classification and with comprehensive labels above the exhibit cases with captions in Latin, French, and English. Its master exhibit of international renown was the mastodon, two skeletons which Peale unearthed in a scientific expedition to New York State in 1801. The museum's 269 portraits and paintings were devoted chiefly to heroes of the American Revolution and founding fathers of the nation. Peale hoped that they would instill love of country in their viewers. A few important naturalists and museum leaders from this country and abroad were also portrayed.

The second major purpose of the museum was to provide what Peale called "rational amusement," which he thought would attract the common people to the museum, also providing its main financial support with their twenty-five-cent admission fees. Peale offered magic mirrors that distorted a viewer into a giant, a dwarf, or a monster with seven heads; a speaking tube mounted in a lion's head that allowed one to shout back and forth with one's friends in another room; a phsiognotrace that would sketch one's silhouette; a pipe organ of eight stops that talented visitors might play; an electrical machine that gave those who touched its extension a moderate shock; and a compound blowpipe to demonstrate the wonders of chemistry. But Peale objected to purely entertaining activities that did not further his educational purpose; he deplored his son Rubens' use of Signor Hellene from Italy, an itinerant one-man band who played the viola, turkish cymbals, tenor drum, Pandean pipes, and Chinese bells.

Another son, Rembrandt, in 1814 estab-

Bald Eagle

Museum of Comparative Zoology,
Harvard University
Photo by Bob Creamer

This mounted eagle is one of 14 birds from Charles
Willson Peale's Philadelphia Museum which were
displayed in "Mermaids, Mummies, and Mastodons."
Of more than 1,600 originally displayed by Peale, only
52 have survived. The eagle appears in the upper left
corner of The Artist in His Museum (page 78).

lished the Peale Museum in Baltimore, which Rubens eventually took over. This structure remains today, the oldest museum building in the country. Rembrandt ran a mainly serious museum with emphasis on art; Rubens offered more and more pure amusement features but failed financially, and Phineas Taylor Barnum ultimately secured the collection, as he did that of Rubens's later museum in New York.

Most American museums stressed entertainment during the period 1800-1870; for example, Joseph Dorfeuille in Cincinnati and Adolph Koch in St. Louis, even though scientists, were compelled to play down their serious interests and devise dramatic shows, such as "The Regions," a frightful panorama of hell, in order to remain solvent. Well-educated British and German travelers found that museums in most American cities were conducted by very unlearned men who tried to make money by presenting serpents, stuffed animals, and waxwork figures, as well as farces, dances, and vaudeville-like acts.

Starting about 1840, Barnum became the leading figure in this entertainment museum world. With humorous hocum and ingenious public relations, he promoted his museums' amusement features but somewhat neglected their scientific contributions; thus the Fiji mermaid was much better known than the exotic animals brought back by his expeditions or his first-rate aquarium. After three disastrous fires had destroyed his collections, he devoted himself to the circus from about 1870. By that time more serious museums of natural history, history, and art began to come to the fore, such as the Smithsonian Institution in Washington, the American Mu-

seum of Natural History, the Metropolitan Museum of Art in New York, the Museum of Fine Arts in Boston, and the Chicago Historical Society. American museums today retain their entertaining activities (lectures, workshops, concerts, performing arts, first-person presentations, and other participatory pursuits), but they are used to enhance the collection and its interpretation, not for non-relevant amusement.

This exhibition showed well the evolution of the American museum as outlined above. It appealed to and even thrilled a large audience with its enlarged Titian Peale's drawing of the Long Room, his father's self-portrait raising the curtain in his museum, the actual mastodon bones and the reproduced skeleton hanging in its chains, the painting of the exhumation of the mastodon, and the striking posters showing numerous Natural Curiosities as well as a Menagerie and Aviary. The scores of smaller objects, the printed articles, and the well-chosen labels contained many educational understandings and nuances. The exhibition also let one see what a nineteenth-century museum looked like and instructed the public on the purposes of a good museum today.

The whole show was successful because of the careful planning and research that went into it. Its main audience consisted of visitors from the Baltimore area and of local school classes admitted free of charge. The printed book, of which this essay is a part, now aims to share the research base of the exhibition with both Baltimoreans and a broader national audience. ❈ ❈ ❈

Entrepreneurs and Intellectuals: Natural History in Early American Museums

Sally Gregory Kohlstedt[1]

The Exhumation of the Mastodon *(left)*
By Charles Willson Peale, 1806-08
Baltimore City Life Museums

Charles Willson Peale memorialized his historic discovery of the first nearly complete skeleton of the extinct mastodon in this painting. With his arm outstretched and family members beside him, Peale supervises the operation while holding a drawing of the front leg.

During the tumultuous and forward looking years following the American Revolution, many articulate citizens argued that the study of natural science was related in fundamental ways to the future of the new republic. Charles Willson Peale, for example, wrote enthusiastically that "Natural History has [a tendency] to promote National and Individual happiness," and he was supported in this assertion by such politically powerful friends as Thomas Jefferson. Indeed, educated citizens discussed natural history in their parlors, promoted public lectures on chemistry and natural philosophy, corresponded with foreign savants, and created local membership societies to collect and display specimens and apparatus. In Philadelphia leaders hoped to retain their city as a political capital, but, failing that, they were determined to reinforce its prominent position in the cultural life of the new nation. The extensive activity in natural history and philosophy contributed to the broad based public underpinning of science and technology in nineteenth century America.[2]

Prominent features of the scientific landscape were the scientific collections acquired by private individuals, by entrepreneurs, by learned academies, by reform communities, by geological surveys, and by specialized study societies. The relative influence among these types of collections varied from the 1790s to the 1850s, but each had a role to play. In the early years, small cabinets were common and reflected a broad and diffuse enthusiasm. Gradually particular practices were more formalized and individual efforts were consolidated. Two distinctive museum patterns emerged during the first half of the nineteenth century. One model was that of the entrepreneurs for whom a museum was also a means of livelihood, and the other involved the specialized natural history societies whose amateur members pooled intellectual resources and artifacts.

The Early Entrepreneurs

Charles Willson Peale and his children reflected and promoted a contemporary outlook which emphasized the importance of educating citizens and exploring the topography of the new nation. Charles W. Peale was an amateur at a time when the term implied serious study that was spurred by a deep interest in a subject rather than by economic incentives. Plants, animals, rocks, fossils, Native American artifacts—such objects and others attracted the attention of men and women who hoped their leisure efforts would have some social or intellectual value. Essentially all training for the study of natural history came through informal means, most often by the encouragement of family members and close friends, or through public lectures, local societies, handbooks, or even the special efforts of an unusual teacher. For many people, however, the motives were complex. A systematic collection of natural history objects could put an active naturalist in touch with an educated class of people, provide some small compensation from a wealthy collector, assist an individual in creating a credential for paid work on a state survey, or even compensate for a less than intellectually gratifying paid position.[3] For Peale, then, and for many others, the pursuit of science was spurred by multiple incentives including profit.

From the moment that the patriarch Charles Willson Peale decided to change his practice of naming his children after painters—Rembrandt, Rubens, Titian, and Sophanisba—to naming them after natural historians and philosophers—Benjamin Franklin and Linnaeus—his personal and economic commitment to scientific study was established. He caught the contemporary enthusiasm for natural history and pursued it through expeditions to collect for his museum. In turn, he provided entertainment and a resource for others who used his collections for study and illustration.

Having decided to establish a museum in Philadelphia, Peale himself took up the tasks of collector, curator, administrator, and educator. His collections emphasized North American materials, those that Peale could collect for himself and those that others contributed, but he also had a store of rare and exotic specimens and artifacts gathered through exchange and donation. His own irrepressible spirit of adventure took him into the field to collect insects and small game. His son Titian Ramsey Peale specialized for a time in butterflies. The most ambitious project and well publicized expedition of the elder Peale, however, resulted in the exhumation of mastodon bones in 1802 from the lower Hudson River valley. The dramatic event also estab-

A Timeline of The Peale Family, 1814–1829

This timeline illustrates events in the lives of the Peale family during the period that the Baltimore museum was managed in turn by Rembrandt and Rubens Peale.

1814

August 15
The Peale Museum in Baltimore opens as "an elegant rendevous for taste, curiosity, and leisure." It features the skeleton of a "mamoth," or mastodon, paintings, natural objects, and Indian relics.

Late August
As Baltimoreans brace for a British attack, Rembrandt Peale finds "it impossible to shoot at a human being" and declines to bear arms.

Top left:
Cap of spruce roots embroidered with grass
   Tlingit, southern Alaska

Top right:
Model of lady's foot, with shoes
   China

Bottom left:
Male figure
   Easter Island

Bottom right:
Hat
   Nootka Sound

American sailors were a source of artifacts from distant cultures, which the Peales exhibited for a curious public. The items illustrated here are among those which have survived from Charles Willson Peale's collection, having passed through the hands of Moses Kimball of the Boston Museum to the Peabody Museum of Archaeology and Ethnology at Harvard University.

1815

October 25
Michael Angelo, eighth child of Rembrandt and Eleanor May Short Peale, is born in Baltimore.

July 4
Rembrandt Peale helps prepare for the laying of the Washington Monument cornerstone by hastily painting a full-length portrait of the first president for display at the ceremony.

Late summer
Charles Willson Peale visits The Peale Museum in Baltimore for the first time.
Winter
With the help of his father Rubens Peale begins installing an elaborate "gas factory" at The Peale Museum in Philadelphia.

lished his prominence among naturalists in America and abroad. One skeleton, painstakingly mounted using scaffold, artificial sections, and a fabricated iron support, was initially on display in the great hall of the American Philosophical Society of Philadelphia, while a second was sent to Europe on tour with his sons. Peale's success in creating large, dramatic exhibits were, perhaps inevitably, imitated by subsequent museum proprietors from New York to St. Louis.[4]

Equally impressive, however, were his experiments with presentation of materials, in art and science, once he had acquired the upper rooms of Independence Hall for exhibition purposes. Here he could imagine a large national museum, perhaps comparable to the Jardin des Plantes, and experiment with display techniques, following the European style of wooden shelves and cases. Perhaps it was his artistic sensibility that persuaded him to think creatively about presentation. To single out natural history as a separate entity in the museum seemed to distort the rich, complex sensibility that Peale, like his contemporaries, had toward art, science, and the environment.

Art was combined with natural history not only by the display of Peale's paintings but also by the special backdrops he created for some of his mounted specimens. At the end of the gallery he created a natural environment. Against a painted background, he built an earthen mound complete with trees and a thicket, and offset by a small pond and beach. Shells and rocks were placed among the mounted mammals, reptiles, amphibians, and a lovely array of birds. Some of the birds appeared to be swimming on the water, others suspended as if flying and still others were perched on branches. His peaceable kingdom was an effort to please his audience with a sketch of landscape and to demonstrate something of the behavior and habitats of the animals on display.[5]

As a curator, Peale concentrated on elements of preservation and security. A prominently posted sign warned, "Do not touch the birds as they are covered with arsenic Poison." The museum enterprise required his constant attention and promotion, since admission fees constituted his family's living. Nonetheless, he realized that his specimens served not

1816

April
The brilliance of gas lighting draws immense crowds to The Peale Museum in Philadelphia. Within weeks, Rubens recoups the $5,000 it cost him to install the gasworks.

October 26
Baltimore's City Council commissions Rembrandt Peale to paint portraits of the heroes of the Battle of Baltimore; Edward Johnson, Samuel Smith, John Stricker, and George Armistead.

Far left: General Samuel Smith; Left: General John Stricker; by Rembrandt Peale

only for edification of a general public but also for scientific enterprise. Indeed, many local Philadelphia naturalists based their descriptions and illustrations on his holdings. Alexander Wilson's pioneering volumes on *American Ornithology* are among the more outstanding examples. Eventually, of course, well illustrated books were an informal competition to museum display, but in the early decades of the nineteenth century the success of Peale's rational amusement served as an evident model to other proprietary enterprises.[6]

Many displays of curiosities and scientific apparatus were quite ephemeral and moved from town to town, but the most ambitious showmen sought to establish permanent facilities, regarding their ultimate goal as an establishment comparable to that of Peale. David Bowen, for example, had opened a waxworks in Philadelphia, but then moved to Boston in 1795 "to avoid a continued competition with my particular friend Charles W. Peale, a distinguished artist."[7] The opening and continuous expansion of his Boston Museum permitted him to create an exhibition with some striking similarities to that of Peale, including

a carved skeleton of a mammoth that he claimed was "an exact model from Mr. Peale's Original Skeleton."[8] After a number of difficulties, including fires and problems with leases, Bowen returned to Philadelphia where he opened a panorama. Parts of his collection were eventually made part of a consolidated New England Museum in 1825, where proprietor E. A. Greenwood combined them with art and natural history specimens from Edward Savage's New-York Museum and the New Haven collection of John Mix. In New York City, too, there were a number of independent enterprises at the turn of the century, several of which were eventually combined by John Scudder in his American Museum at the base of Manhattan Island in 1817. Rembrandt Peale's Baltimore Museum, of course, similarly drew on his father's establishment. The pattern of numerous individual initiatives gradually consolidated in larger and more comprehensive museums became familiar as the popular museum effort followed westward migration. The 1820s were a high point in enthusiasm for such phenomena along the Atlantic Coast.

Right: Mayor Edward Johnson; Far right: Lt. Colonel Armistead; by Rembrandt Peale

1817

December 25-late April 1818
Naturalist Titian Ramsey Peale II, ornithologist George Ord, naturalist Thomas Say, and geologist William Maclure explore Spanish Florida for several months, observing and collecting plants and animals.

Titian Peale by Charles Willson Peale

Feather headdress, on coarse netting
Carib or Arawak, South America
Peabody Museum of Archaeology and Ethnology,
Harvard University

The Naturalists and their Collections

The necessity of attracting and retaining a paying audience had left entrepreneurs like Peale and Scudder little time to pursue the study of natural history or to develop the kinds of reference collections increasingly preferred by naturalists. By the 1810s, serious amateurs began to create societies through which they could build cabinets and museums, share scientific information, and produce publications.

The incentives of the naturalists carried some of the nationalism that had spurred Thomas Jefferson to challenge European naturalists like Count Buffon. The Frenchman had indicated in his *Natural History of Man* that the American environment, with its irregular topography and variability in weather, produced animals (including native peoples) that were smaller and less vigorous than those of Europe. Jefferson's *Notes on Virginia* provided one adamant retort and his compatriots sought scientific evidence about American flora and fauna which they expected would refute such European prejudices.[9] In their investigation they followed the descriptive and taxonomic methods which characterized European research. In the era of exploration and colonization, the collections of data from around the world led to new theoretical arguments about the distribution and development of species. The Americas had much to contribute to the discussion.

The naturalists who studied and collected natural history objects typically shared a commitment to self-improvement, group collaboration, and national advancement. They created local societies to link the layers of individual activity—private conversations, semi-private correspondence, exchange of specimens, and presentation of ideas—into a collaborative project to identify and map all species in the American landscape. Their work was part of an international taxonomic enterprise. Larger cities were typically the center for new societies, and individuals on the periphery were connected via correspondence and publications.

In the eighteenth century learned societies were broadly defined. The Charles Town Library Society, founded in 1773, acquired natural specimens and natural artifacts as well

1818

Rubens Peale publishes a handbill boasting of the vast holdings of the Peale Museum in Philadelphia: 1,240 birds, 212 animals, 121 fishes, 1,044 shells, 8,000 minerals, and 180 portraits.

November
Sarah Miriam Peale, Rembrandt's cousin and a budding painter, visits The Peale Museum in Baltimore, where she later opens a studio.

Self-portrait by Sarah Miriam Peale

Philadelphia Museum label
Peabody Museum of Archaeology and Ethnology, Harvard University

Labels such as this, which refers to the object pictured on the opposite page, provided the basic identification for Peale's many objects and were handwritten, clipped from numbered catalogues, or printed with a fancy border. Donors were often acknowledged on labels.

as books and art objects. Prominent learned societies in such as the American Philosophical Society of Philadelphia and the American Academy of Arts and Sciences in Boston acquired individual items by donation but resisted the idea of a comprehensive museum. During the 1810s, therefore, naturalists in these and other cities drew together and initiated fledgling societies explicitly for the study of natural history.[10]

By mutual accord, these societies almost immediately began to acquire specimens and to plan for permanent facilities to house them. In Philadelphia, individual members of the Academy of Natural Sciences originally maintained separate cases for their personal collections, while the young members of the short-lived Worcester Natural History Society contributed to a set of mutual holdings. Regardless of formal ownership, the collections were to be shared in the study of taxonomic systems and as a reference point for unidentified specimens. In fact, a New York group named itself for Carl Linnaeus, the Swedish naturalist who had developed the Latin based, international binomial nomenclature for flora

and fauna. The natural history societies stated their primary goal as research and the advancement of knowledge. Specimens of minerals, plants, and specialized groups of snakes, insects, butterflies, mammals and other creatures were carefully identified and systematically arranged in order to emphasize their relationship to each other or, sometimes, their geographical origin.

Philadelphia's Academy of Natural Sciences was one of the earliest and most successful of such societies. The sustaining financial sponsorship and intellectual vision of William McClure, a Scottish immigrant, underscored the Academy's international connections and cultural base. Another immigrant from France, Charles Alexander LeSueur, travelled with McClure to the West Indies and then returned to work in Philadelphia as art teacher, illustrator, and curator at the Academy. Many of the early Academy members used Peale's collections in order to illustrate their pioneering books, such as Wilson's *American Ornithology*. Titian Ramsey Peale drew illustrations for the books of Charles Lucian Bonaparte, and Peale's son-in-

1819

February
While visiting Baltimore, Charles Willson Peale acquires a "fast walking machine," or bicycle. The fast-walking craze soon leads to laws prohibiting its use in Philadelphia.

Baltimore's City Council commissions a fifth painting by Rembrandt Peale, a posthumous portrait of Joshua Barney. The Revolutionary War naval hero died in December 1818.

Commodore Joshua Barney by Rembrandt Peale

Carolina Parrot
mounted before 1811
Museum of Comparative Zoology,
Harvard University
American Ornithology (Volume 3) by Alexander
Wilson (Philadelphia, 1811)
Library, The Academy of Natural Sciences of
Philadelphia
Photo by Bob Creamer

Alexander Wilson's nine volume work was the first book about American birds. Wilson drew many of the book's illustrations using specimens displayed at Peale's Philadelphia museum, including the Carolina Parrot, a bird extinct since 1914.

1820

April

Artist William Dunlap visits the studios of Rembrandt Peale, Thomas Sully, and Jacob Eicholtz. Unimpressed by Peale, he admires Sully's work and notes that the lesser-known Eicholtz has produced more work than the others.

1821

Summer

Novelty entertainments—immensely popular with the public but disliked by Charles Willson Peale—invade the Peale Museum in Philadelphia. Signor Hellene, a one-man band, is a profitable attraction after his appearance at The Peale Museum in Baltimore.

October

A yellow fever epidemic in Philadelphia afflicts Charles Willson Peale, and takes the life of Hannah Peale, his wife.

Right: Hannah Peale,
by Charles Willson Peale

law John Godman used the museum in order to illustrate his *American Natural History*. The Philadelphia naturalists, in fact, were among the most published zoologists and geologists in the young nation. The Academy's own collections were strongest in those objects most easy to transport or in which prominent members had special interests, such as the minerals of Dr. Seybert, the shell collection of explorer Stephen H. Long, the insects of Thomas Say, and the birds of Alexander Wilson and his son. The members very quickly established an exchange of specimens with similar societies in Europe for duplicate specimens and journal publications. Increasingly in the 1820s and 1830s, they made contact with colleagues in Boston, New York, Charleston, Pittsburgh, Cincinnati, and St. Louis. A generation of younger scholars could use the facilities of such semi-private societies to become experts and specialists and thus seek a career in science. Asa Gray, for example, worked with John Torrey at the New York Lyceum of Natural History, gaining an expertise that served him well as head of Harvard's herbarium. Cataloging and organizing these collections by scientific type left little time for working on displays. From Boston to Charleston, the presentation and displays of natural history collections varied widely, sometimes arranged in individual cabinets by donor, by species, or by geographic origins of the specimens.

Natural history society members consistently emphasized new discoveries, thorough and detailed descriptions, and international recognition for scientific work as their first priority. Published discussions about classification underscored the scientific value of museum holdings. Like the entrepreneurs, however, members of the societies found it difficult to maintain and manage large and complex collections. The ongoing threats of fire and theft were both very real, but more persistent were the expenses of maintaining the buildings, of preserving fragile specimens, and of motivating the voluntary contributions of time from local members needed to manage the growing collections. Only a few of the early societies prospered more than a few years. The bankruptcy of the New York Lyceum after the Panic of 1837 reminded other

1822

January
Rembrandt Peale, in poor health and longing for time to paint, urges his brother Rubens to take over The Peale Museum in Baltimore.

March
Rubens Peale prepares to leave Philadelphia to manage The Peale Museum in Baltimore. His retired father, Charles Willson Peale, agrees to manage The Peale Museum in Philadelphia. Rembrandt and his family move to New York in the spring.

Late July–September 10
Charles Willson Peale paints his autobiographical self-portrait, *The Artist in His Museum*.

Mermaid

Peabody Museum of Archaeology and Ethnology
Harvard University
Photo by Bob Creamer

The manufacture of mermaids was a nineteenth century Japanese craft. P.T. Barnum's exhibition of one such artifact as an authentic curiosity of nature attracted not only large crowds to his museum, but also the wrath of natural scientists.

1823

January
Rembrandt Peale decides he must go to London to attract new patrons, and for much of the year tries unsuccessfully to raise the necessary funds.

Spring
Charles Willson Peale's lecture series on natural history at The Peale Museum in Philadelphia stirs little public interest.

Right: Self-Portrait,
by Charles Willson Peale

December
Rembrandt Peale begins a new portrait of George Washington, a work he calls the *Standard Likeness of Washington.*

Figuratively, P.T. Barnum was heir to the Peales, acquiring the contents of Rubens Peale's New York museum in 1842, leasing the Baltimore museum in 1845 and 1846, and purchasing a portion of the contents of the Philadelphia museum in 1850.

younger natural history societies of the risks involved in building facilities and maintaining them.

Troubled Times for Museums

In the 1830s and 1840s, both proprietary museums and those of urban natural history societies faced practical and intellectual difficulties. To some extent, they both faced the challenges of basic maintenance and of creating coherent and useful displays. At the same time, there were increasing tensions as each kind of museum took a distinctive path.

Proprietary museum directors responded to box office problems by adding such attractions as theater, music, and popular entertainment. The efforts of Charles Willson Peale and his sons to add amusements to their museums in Philadelphia, New York, and Baltimore initially brought financial success. In Baltimore, for example, Rembrandt Peale used piped gas lighting to dramatic effect and to introduce the possibility of gas lighting for the city. When Rubens Peale took over in 1823, he added curios—an Egyptian mummy, Chinese chopsticks, coins, and medals— and a live menagerie that featured an imported ti-

ger as well as such native wildlife as alligators, wolves, and rattlesnakes. But presenting the museum as an entertainment center meant that the Peales faced a different competition. As Rubens ruefully commented, "Since the opening of the circus I have been completely deserted."[11]

Moreover, the relatively congenial relationship between local naturalists and proprietors represented by the Academy of Natural Sciences and Peale's museum in Philadelphia had begun to decline. Naturalists who had enjoyed free admission to Scudder's museum or who depended on specimens in Peale's museum wanted the collections to improve in scientific terms of quality and complexity and were often appalled by the apparent shift toward mere amusement. Often, they suspected, quite the opposite of scientific investigation lurked behind entertainment and the hoopla of showmen like P. T. Barnum.

In one of the more dramatic examples of the conflict, the scientists took on Barnum in the early 1840s. Most of his discoveries had in fact been found by others, but Barnum had the advertising genius to attract and sustain public interest. In 1842 he became part owner

1824

Summer
British taxidermist Charles Waterton visits Charles Willson Peale at The Peale Museum in Philadelphia. He later calls the mastodon "a national treasure."

November–April 1825
Titian Peale travels through Florida collecting bird specimens for Charles-Lucien Bonaparte's forthcoming revision of Alexander Wilson's pioneering work on birds.

Left: Charles Waterton
by Charles Willson Peale

of a "feejee mermaid." The object was not attractive and was described in local newspapers as an "ugly dried-up, block-looking, and diminutive specimen about three feet long. Its mouth was open, its tail turned over, and its arms thrown up, giving it the appearance of having died in great agony." The specimen had tripled revenues at the American Museum in New York City, but as interest there waned Barnum decided to send the mermaid on a tour of the South.

As the mermaid exhibition went from town to town en route to Charleston, a local naturalist, the Reverend John Bachman, using the pseudonym "No Humbug," denounced the specimen as a fraud in local newspapers. The well-known naturalist and collaborator of John James Audubon brought his distinguished South Carolina colleagues, Dr. Lewis R. Gibbes and herpetologist J. Edwards Holbrook, into the debate. Drawing self-consciously on scientific expertise, and determined to debunk the mermaid exhibition, Bachman recommended visiting the exhibit "without making ourselves known and satisfying ourselves of the manner in which the animal has been manufactured." The conclusion

of the naturalists was that the "vice manufacture . . . palmed on our community as a great natural curiosity" had two chests and two abdomens and was scarcely a natural phenomenon.[12] Newspapers picked up on the debate and at least one local newspaper editor sided with Barnum and attacked the "scientifics" who claimed authority without sufficient information. Barnum knew just how to play the experts and confided to a showman in Boston his delight that "every devil among the scientifics would swear that its existence [is] a natural impossibility." To add to the drama he contemplated a "pretend lawsuit" and imagined a scenario which would have the naturalists pay to see the specimen in order to prepare their defense against the charges. Small wonder that the relationship between showmen and naturalists degenerated to a level of mutual contempt.

The disillusion went deeper as scientists expressed their frustration with a public that seemed gullible and, indeed, more attracted to trivial and idle pursuits than to serious scientific matters. Older members of the natural history societies therefore tended to resist younger members or outsiders who asked that

1825

January
Rembrandt Peale displays his painting *Washington Before Yorktown* in the U.S. Capitol, and lobbies for its sale to Congress.

October 26
Rubens Peale opens the Parthenon, his New York museum at 252 Broadway. It features a lecture room "for the exhibition of popular and striking experiments, accompanied with short explanations," and its flat roof affords visitors views of Broadway and the Hudson.

Washington Before Yorktown *by Rembrandt Peale*

they make their societies' collections more accessible to the general public.

By the 1850s, those who had collected and displayed natural history objects faced serious problems. Much of the material collected by the first generation of proprietors had been combined into displays presented in the theater of Moses Kimball in Boston and major exhibition center of P. T. Barnum in New York. There the mounted skins and skeletons were of passing interest but not intended to provide more than short-term amusement. In the quiet halls of the natural history societies, a few members studied the specimens mounted in cases or preserved in drawers, but members had little time or inclination to create educational displays or even to emphasize the aesthetic quality of holdings. Neither type of museum management had made the natural sciences accessible to the broad adult public that increasingly turned to self help books and more formal educational establishments to learn about plants, chemical phenomena, and the solar system. Neither paid any significant attention to children as an important audience. The eclipse of both museum types made way, however, for a quite different approach to museum building in the last half of the century.

Redefining the Museum Enterprise

The early aspirations about the role of natural history museums proved ephemeral, but the legacy of the proprietors and the natural history societies was important. The physical collections were an important resource and the experiences established a base from which to make decisions about the future.

During the last half of the nineteenth century a new philosophy about the importance of museums for education created opportunities in which the skills of those who had run popular museums could be combined with the expertise of geologists, zoologists, and anthropologists. The successful museums in the last half of the century, moreover, gained something that had eluded both proprietors and voluntary members of natural history societies, namely a steady source of support through civic sponsorship. The new model museum would have opportunities for paid curators whose life work was in natural sci-

1826

January
Rembrandt Peale is one of 30 founders of the National Academy of Design.

John D. Godman, grandson-in-law of Charles Willson Peale, publishes the first of his three-volume *American Natural History*. Many illustrations by family friend and colleague Charles Lesueur are based on mounted specimens in The Peale Museum in Philadelphia.

December
In New York, Charles Willson Peale visits an exhibition of live animals that includes an ". . . Elephant, Cammel, Lamma, Lyons, Tygars, Panthers, Bear, Monkie. . . ." Later that month, this tiger escapes and the elephant rescues the animal keeper.

ence, especially those who would also create public displays to arouse an inquisitive public audience.

By mid-century educational reformers and scientists tended to agree that more science should be taught to children. The plans of educational reformers—whether interpreted by revisionist historians who stress the socialization of immigrants, by educational historians who emphasized the noble democratic ideals expressed, or by intellectual historians who concentrated on curriculum—demonstrated considerable interest in providing more education in the natural sciences. Those educational activists like Horace Mann who established teacher training colleges across the country were, moreover, often enamored of the philosophy of Germans like Pestalozzi, Froebel, and others who stressed the effectiveness of "object study." Natural history collections, gathered on class field trips or placed on display in hall cabinets, became part of private and then public school thinking. One of the earliest and best examples was in the German-English Academy in Milwaukee where Peter Englemann sponsored a natural history society in order to develop and sustain an ob-

ject collection. His enterprise was so successful that the principal of the Milwaukee Public High School for that same period, George W. Peckham, also established an assembly room for the study of natural history.[13]

The American scientist who most clearly had learned some of these outlooks was an emigré, Louis Agassiz. His Swiss and German education led him to value teaching with objects. While his career concentrated on collegiate and post-baccalaureate scientific study, Agassiz (perhaps more by example than pedagogical method) trained a generation of men (and even a few women) who led the movement to make collections educational in systematic ways.[14] The example of Alpheus Hyatt at the Boston Society of Natural History suggested some of the ways in which collections could be used for education—beginning with the MIT students in the 1870s but gradually extending to teachers and pupils, and finally working to attract a more general public. He was aided in this effort by Lucretia Crocker, a teacher who had attended the lectures of Agassiz at the Framingham Normal School and eventually became the superintendent of science in the Boston Public Schools. Spurred

1827

February 22
Charles Willson Peale dies in Philadelphia at the age of 85.

May
The Peale Museum in New York advertises a calf with two heads, six legs, and two tails—but "otherwise perfectly formed."

The Arcade, Philadelphia

August
The Peale Museum in Philadelphia moves from Independence Hall to more spacious quarters in the new Arcade.

in part by her initiatives, Hyatt had experimented with hiring guides, had introduced special evening and Saturday classes, produced guidebooks, and added more descriptive charts and posters to displays in order to make the museum an educational institution.[15] Another Agassiz student, Albert Bickmore, became head of the American Museum of Natural History and developed an extensive program to loan boxes of selected specimens to teachers for use in schools, a technique that became widely imitated.

Within the museums the years surrounding the Civil War were difficult. Many of the older societies faced financial hard times and internal dissension about the nature of the museum enterprise. Fundamental questions were asked: What should be collected? Who should do the collecting? What should be displayed? How should displays be organized? How much description should be provided? In what way should materials be described? These questions remain contested even to the present day, but until museums became public institutions, there was little need to debate since individuals and private corporations

tended to reflect patrons' tastes and local inclinations.[16]

By mid-century, however, the preservation and research functions became more explicit and education was to function in some way parallel to the these scientific emphases on collecting, organizing, and studying objects. The scientific museums affiliated with colleges, like Louis Agassiz's Museum of Comparative Zoology at Harvard, were typically described as having two functions, namely research and education. Scientists were often directors as well as curators in the natural history museums established during the middle decades of the century. They promoted an agenda that led to scholarly publications and displays coincident with contemporary classification. The judgment was that of peers.

The didactic possibilities of museum display were evident, however, when curators had the time to attend to this function. Unlike Peale's museum, the displays after 1850 for the most part eschewed monstrosities, abnormalities, and aesthetics in favor of systematic displays of specimens by type, each identified by a label that stressed in clear

---

1828

June 18
Lt. George Hutter gives 35 American Indian artifacts originally collected by the Lewis and Clark expedition to The Peale Museum in Philadelphia. Acquired by Hutter's father from Thomas Jefferson, they join other Lewis and Clark artifacts given to Peale in 1809.

November 26, 1828–October 1830
Rembrandt Peale and son Angelo travel to Italy to study and paint copies of Old Masters. Rembrandt's copies draw praise, as does his *Standard Likeness* of Washington. The trip rejuvenates him after a decade of poor health and disappointments.

Angel by Rembrandt Peale after Corregio

terms the scientific name, habitat, and sometimes observed behavior of the object on display. Museums were intended to be serious institutions, as the Smithsonian had been, for the increase and diffusion of knowledge. However, the mid-century museums were distant and distinct from some of the older society collections in that scientific organization took precedence over personal identification—gone with names and arbitrary division of materials by donor—and there were fewer rules governing who might see the treasures acquired.

Systematic collections became the norm, particularly well established on college campuses by the 1870s. They were intended to be more than a good show or a tribute to the initiative of individuals; now they were part of an activity in which the objects were significant only when used as a demonstration for a classification scheme or in order to represent some scientific principle. Thus on campus, the museum holdings were typically classified and arranged by scientific nomenclature and reflected the interests and expertise of faculty. A few patrons enabled colleges to establish what were considered "comprehensive" museums, such as Vassar College, the University of Virginia, Cornell University, and several state universities.[17]

The serious intentions were rarely fully realized, in part because the museums' programs were an activity negotiated among scientists, teachers, students, and a more general public. By the 1870s, it was clear that a certain amount of drama was essential in attracting public audiences, and their passage through newly developed turnstiles validated the expenditure of public funds. It was, in the case of the Boston Society of Natural History, teachers who brought classes to museums and asked for more and better help in describing and explaining the exhibits. In some cities, politicians suggested that displays be made more attractive and they applauded such innovations as habitat groups that presumably showed animals in their natural environment, and lantern slide shows that illustrated the entire natural world and highlighted the unfamiliar. These devices previously thought of as entertainment could now be justified as having educational value as well.

1829

Along with natural curiosities and painting, The Peale Museum in New York features Indians in January and March, astronomy lectures in February and March, Francis Smith of Baltimore performing on musical glasses in May, two fat girls in June, a ventriloquist in August, a glass blower in September, and Mr. and Mrs. Canderbeck playing the harp and violin in December.

The Parthenon, New York City

While it is possible to identify some apparent "firsts," the striking thing about museum development in the 1870s and 1880s is the extent to which similar activities were initiated almost simultaneously in this country and abroad. The emphasis included, but was not confined to, using display to demonstrate scientific classification. There were still fundamental debates about classification and nomenclature, however, and that disagreement meant that different institutions made different arrangements. Minerals might be displayed on the basis of traditional geological typology, as in many antebellum collegiate collections, or on the basis of their chemical components, as James Dwight Dana attempted at Yale. Zoological specimens might be displayed by type, or in some cases by geographical origin, a technique best demonstrated at the University of Melbourne in Australia. Sponsors and donors as well as the scientific curators could dictate actual practice. In Chicago, for example, the donation of wood samples and money to display them in a "practical way" led to a demonstration of wood by use rather than any biological scheme at Field's Columbian Museum in the 1890s.

By the end of the century, the difficulties of defining the function and the organization of museums led to more discussion among those who worked in museums. The Smithsonian Institution's associate director for the United States National Museum, George Brown Goode, was well-positioned to develop a theoretical base. In the first of the Smithsonian's Circulars, he identified three principle roles for major museums: museum of record, museum of research, and educational museum. The efficient educational museum might be "described as a collection of instructive labels, each illustrated by a well-selected specimen."[18] In some scientific museums this view would dominate for a century, but others would find themselves doing even more to renegotiate the role of affective and dramatic demonstrations and displays, including elephants in front lobbies and or entire museum wings given over to African, Asian, or other places exotic to America. These were more typically "draws" intended to bring people in so that they would "learn" from the other more systematic presentations. Often, in fact, there was relatively little written material to accompany these special features.

The process of creating museums by the later nineteenth century culminated when curators and patrons found a new balance among the functions of preservation, research, and public education. By then, some of the skills of an entrepreneur and public educator like Charles Willson Peale had been combined with the expertise of a naturalist like Asa Gray. The museum had become a place for tell and show. ❊ ❊ ❊

🎋 In Pursuit of a Profit

John W. Durel

Rubens Peale in 1830 moved his museum collections to "a more central and more suitable situation" amidst the hurly-burly of Baltimore's principal commercial thoroughfare. The museum occupied the upper floors of this prominent building; the first floor housed an arcade of shops.

Against the advice of his father, but following his father's example, Rembrandt Peale opened a "Museum and Gallery of the Fine Arts" in 1814 in Baltimore, the third largest city in the young American republic. Baltimore had arrived on the scene later than Philadelphia and New York, but rapid growth after the Revolution placed it in the top rank. By the time Rembrandt opened his museum, the city boasted a strong commercial economy, a large and diverse population, and a host of cultural and social institutions. In spite of his father's arguments to the contrary, Rembrandt had good reason to believe that his museum venture would succeed.

For the next 15 years, from 1814 to 1829, first Rembrandt and then his brother Rubens, operated "Peale's Museum" on Holliday Street. They created a museum much like Charles Willson Peale's in Philadelphia, presenting to the public an array of man-made and natural curiosities, including a mastodon skeleton, complemented by scientific demonstrations and other "rational amusement."

Through surviving correspondence and records we can glimpse Rembrandt and Rubens at work as museum "directors." For example, on a fall evening in 1818 we see Rembrandt frustrated because his gas supply has failed, disappointing the many visitors who had come to see the museum's novel gas lighting; the next morning, after a lady sits for a portrait, he is off to a local newspaper office to advertise other museum events scheduled for that evening and the next; in the evening we see him performing scientific experiments and giving a magic lantern show. [1] We encounter, to use modern parlance, a typical director of a small museum, who works as curator, educator, marketing director, and even projectionist!

Unlike most modern museums, the Peale Museum was a private enterprise, operated to make a profit. In addition to Rembrandt, and later Rubens, there were five stockholders who expected an 8 percent return on their investments. Thus, the Peales had to earn, primarily through admissions income, enough money to meet operating expenses, support themselves, and pay dividends.

In the timeline which follows, thanks to meticulous records kept by Rubens, we can trace the museum's revenue over the course of fifteen years, month by month and some-

Robert Cary Long, Sr. *(1770-1833)*
Oil on canvas, 19th Century
Copy after Rembrandt Peale
Baltimore City Life Museums

Talented and ambitious, Robert Cary Long, Sr. rose from carpenter's apprentice to building contractor to Baltimore's leading native-born architect.

Museum and Gallery of the Fine Arts
Engraving by Joseph Cone; published in Thomas H Poppleton's "Plan of the City of Baltimore . . . 1823."
Baltimore City Life Museums

This was the first building in America designed as a museum. Having no precedent to guide him, architect Robert Cary Long, Sr. elevated the traditional five-bay federal house to the status of public monument through his use of an imposing central pavilion.

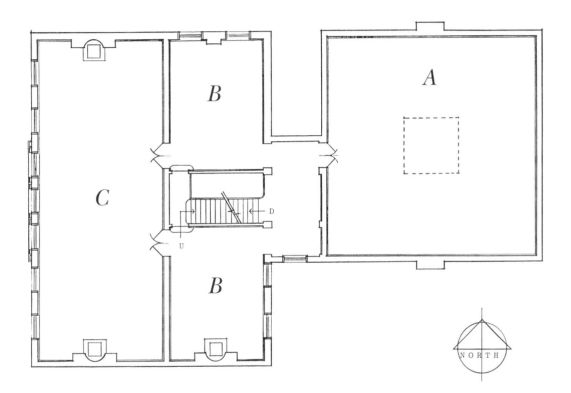

Plan of Second Floor, Peale's Baltimore Museum, ca.1814
Conjectural drawing by James T. Wollon, AIA, June 1992.
A. Picture Gallery measuring 35 feet square.
B. Side rooms, one of which probably housed the mastodon.
C. Front room probably used as a lecture hall and music room.

Above all, Rembrandt Peale was proud of his large "Picture Gallery" attached to the new museum. There he displayed his portraits of statesmen and generals alongside the allegorical Roman Daughter *and* King Lear.

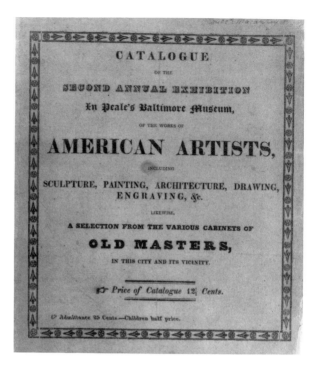

Rubens Peale borrowed from local collectors and solicited new paintings from his own family and professional friends for an annual art exhibition in Baltimore. Children were admitted for half the 25-cent adult fee. The exhibition helped to boost fall admissions revenue.

times even week by week.[2] It is easy to discern the strong positive correlation between special events and increases in attendance. Revenue peaked with such attractions as the exhibition of Rembrandt's allegorical painting, *The Court of Death*, in 1820; the night-blooming of the rare *Cactus triangularis* in 1822; and the appearance of the trained dog, Apollo, in 1828.

Because of the novelty of gas lighting, revenue was greatest in the evening. Under Rembrandt's direction, the museum was open six days a week, Sundays excepted, and some evenings. Rubens, upon taking over in 1822, quickly understood that he "would do but little if it were not for the nights," and extended evening opening to all six days.[3] Permanent exhibits, such as the mastodon skeleton, were not enough to sustain the museum. Special events, usually offered in the evening, were essential to success.

The Peale Museum competed with other museums and attractions for the attention and money of Baltimoreans. The timeline gives a sampling of competing cultural and entertainment events. Sometimes the competition hurt. In August, 1822 Rubens complained that "these last 3 days have been very close and sultry, scarcely anybody moving and the Williams are playing at the Pavilion at 25 cents each visitor, giving them a play and dancing on slack and tight ropes &c &c &c." In December he wrote "since the opening of the circus I have been completely deserted all run mad after Mr. Hunter and as soon as the genteel part quit it they have taken to the small theatre. . . ."[4]

Still, as the timeline makes clear, the Peales had their successes. The year 1824 stands out as especially productive. The summer season began with an exhibition of the first human mummy brought to America. Given as a gift to the Massachusetts General Hospital, "this curious relic of Antiquity" toured the Atlantic seaboard in 1823 and 1824. Rubens arranged to have it shown at the museum from June 14 to July 24, for a fee of $650 plus transportation expenses of $79.75. The residents of Baltimore eagerly paid their quarters to see the mummy, and during the run Rubens took in $2,502.02 from admissions and the sale of mineral waters and fruit. [5]

In the fall there were more successes. In September, on the 10th anniversary of the Battle of Baltimore, a large crowd came to hear music and see a "transparency" of George Washington. The visit of the Marquis de Lafayette in October yielded the largest weekly attendance in fifteen years. The third annual art exhibit, opening later that month, also attracted many visitors.

However, the achievements of 1824 mask the serious financial difficulties that the museum faced. A year earlier Charles Willson Peale had advised Rubens to cease making improvements to the museum and to pay off the stockholders. But the younger museum entrepreneur was ambitious. He defended his expenses and sought new opportunities, including the possibility of linking the museum to a nearby shot tower, which stood about 160 feet high. Museum visitors would be able to climb to the top for a view of the city, and the tower itself would serve as a beacon to attract visitors.[6] Although this scheme did not materialize, it shows that Rubens, in 1823, saw the solution to his financial problems not in curtailed expenses but in increased revenue.

☙ *The Court of Death*
  By Rembrandt Peale, 1820
  The Detroit Institute of Arts
  Gift of George H. Scripps

*Attendance peaked at Rembrandt Peale's Baltimore
Museum when he exhibited this great allegorical
painting in September of 1820.*

The Egyptian Mummy
Outer Coffin of the Mummy Padihershef
Museum of Fine Arts, Springfield, Mass.
Photo by Bob Creamer

The first Egyptian human mummy to cross the Atlantic visited Peale's Baltimore Museum in 1824. Promoted as "The Egyptian Mummy," it was soon followed by many others, so that within a year there were complaints that the market was glutted. Rubens Peale was fortunate to catch the first wave of excitement and turned a profit. Before long mummies were commonplace in museums and eventually relegated to side galleries and storage rooms.

By the summer of 1824, even as the Egyptian mummy was earning him a substantial profit, Rubens had changed his mind. In August he decided to give up the museum, lamenting to his brother Rembrandt that "I have used every exertion to make the income a good one, and with all this it will not pay its way and give me a moderate living." In September, amidst preparations for the forthcoming visit of General Lafayette he met with the museum stockholders and offered his resignation. Although some accommodation was reached at that time, the following year he moved to New York to open a museum there.[7]

Rubens left the care of the Baltimore museum in the hands of a salaried manager. The museum stayed at the Holliday Street location until 1829, when it moved to a more central location. It continued to struggle financially, and in 1835 Rubens sold his interest in the enterprise.

As an executive director (again to use modern terms) Rubens Peale was ambitious and talented. Like many directors of small museums today, he juggled a number of jobs while serving both the public and the museum's board. He studied his audience, cared for the collections, believed in what he was doing, and paid the bills most of the time. Today's museums directors can identify easily with the challenges he faced.

However, museum visitors seldom are interested in the trials of the museum's director. They come to see the exhibits and enjoy the demonstrations. The timeline offers readers an opportunity to explore the wondrous "beasts, birds, pictures, paintings, & all curiosities natural & artificial" found in "Peale's Baltimore Museum situate in Holliday Street."[8] Enjoy your tour! ❈ ❈ ❈

✤ A Timeline of Peale's Baltimore Museum, 1814–1829

This timeline illustrates many of the activities in the Peale Museum under the management of Rembrandt and Rubens Peale, and offers a sampling of competing cultural and entertainment events. Monthly income records from 1814 to 1821 and weekly records thereafter help estimate attendance.

1814–1821. *Rembrandt Peale operated this museum as a private business for profit. He charged adults 25 cents admission, and half-price for children; the Peale Museum was open every day except Sunday and some evenings.*

1822–1829. *Rubens Peale, like Rembrandt, operated the museum as a private business for profit. He charged adults 25 cents and half-price for children; the museum was now open every day and evening except Sunday.*

opposite:
The Peale Museum, 1990
Baltimore City Life Museums

1 8 1 4

Income $1,755.10 (August–December)

Income

$1200
$1150
$1100
$1050
$1000
$950
$900
$850
$800
$750
$700
$650
$600
$550
$500
$450
$400
$350
$300
$250
$200
$150
$100
$50
$0

July 4
*The Baltimore museum at
Market and Sharp Streets
advertises a leopard, a tiger,
a seahorse, whale bones, live
birds, 21 wax figures, and
electrical machines.
Silhouettes sell for 25 cents.*

July 30
*Elisha Gray, a 3-ft., 2-in.,
dwarf, may be seen at
Clark's Tavern for 25 cents.*

August 15
*The Peale Museum in
Baltimore opens as "an
elegant rendevous for taste,
curiosity, and leisure." It
features the skeleton of a
"mammoth," or mastodon,
paintings, natural history
objects, and Indian relics.*

September 12–14
*In the Battle of Baltimore, a
citizens' militia repels land
and sea attacks by the
British. Inspired by the
valiant defense of Fort
McHenry, Francis Scott Key
writes "The Star-Spangled
Banner."*

November 29
*New evening hours on
Tuesdays and Thursdays
bring more visitors to The
Peale Museum.*

Rembrandt Peale's estimate of annual expenses

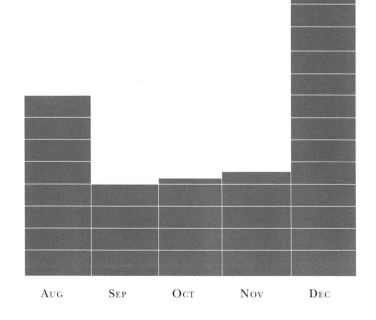

AUG   SEP   OCT   NOV   DEC

1 8 1 5

Income

$1200
$1150
$1100
$1050
$1000
$950
$900
$850
$800
$750
$700
$650
$600
$550
$500
$450
$400
$350
$300
$250
$200
$150
$100
$50
$0

THE AFRICAN LION
TO BE SEEN AT THE
Baltimore Museum.

Corner of Lexington & Howard streets.
Encouraged by the most generous citizens in the world, the proprietor of the Baltimore Museum, has recently added several thousand Mechanical and Natural Curiosities. Among which are a large EAGLE alive, a large collection of Wax Figures and Paintings, as large as life ; Rockets, Bomb Shells, etc. of every description, thrown into Baltimore, during the bombardment, several electrical machines. Visitors operated on gratis, and afflcte† †persons visited at their houses, and machines hired out.
The Museum is open from 6 in the Morning until 10 in the Evening. Admittance 25 cents—children half price.
Persons who present curio-ities admitted gratis. PROFILES cut, framed and painted at the museum.
A variety of Paintings of naked beauties, as large as life, from Paris, are exhibited in a separate room. Admittance 25 cents.

aug 25   law

January 8
Gen. Andrew Jackson's motley American forces defeat 7,500 British troops at the Battle of New Orleans; neither side knew the War of 1812 had ended on Christmas Eve

February 16
To celebrate the end of the War of 1812, "a beautiful emblematic transparency was exhibited in front of Mr. Peale's Museum, representing the angel of peace hovering over the American Eagle which was in the act of receiving the olive branch from a dove."

May 1
The Peale Museum now includes Rembrandt Peale's historical paintings Napoleon on Horseback, King Lear in the Tempest, *and* The Roman Daughter.

Summer
A museum at Lexington and Howard Streets promises paintings of "naked beauties, as large as life, from Paris" for just 25 cents admission. Donors of curiosities are admitted free. The rival Columbian Museum at the Fountain Hotel advertises that "Smoking Segars" is not permitted.

The Roman Daughter
by Rembrandt Peale

JAN   FEB   MAR   APR   MAY   JUN   JUL   AUG   SEP   OCT   NOV   DEC

1 8 1 6

Income $7,195.00

Income

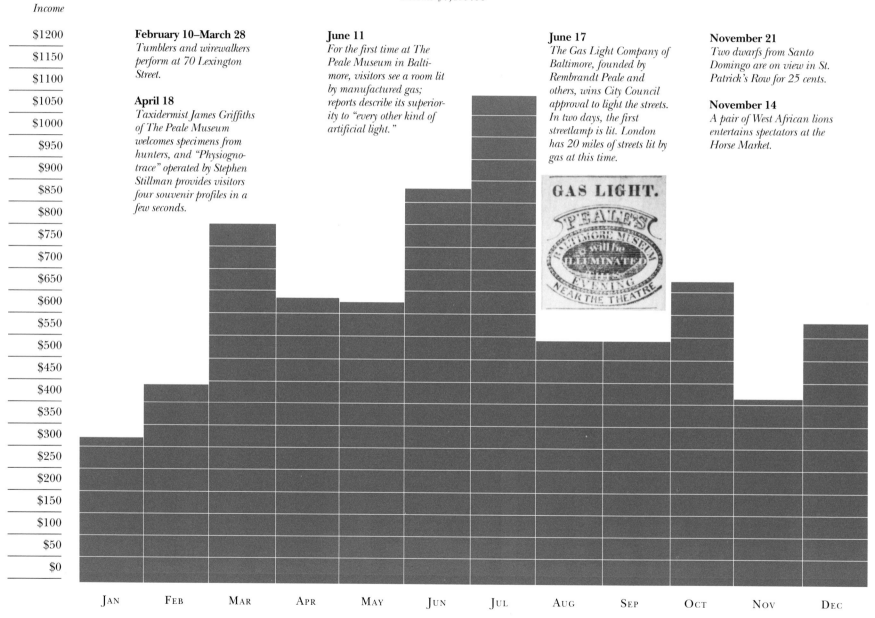

February 10–March 28
Tumblers and wirewalkers perform at 70 Lexington Street.

April 18
Taxidermist James Griffiths of The Peale Museum welcomes specimens from hunters, and "Physiogno-trace" operated by Stephen Stillman provides visitors four souvenir profiles in a few seconds.

June 11
For the first time at The Peale Museum in Baltimore, visitors see a room lit by manufactured gas; reports describe its superiority to "every other kind of artificial light."

June 17
The Gas Light Company of Baltimore, founded by Rembrandt Peale and others, wins City Council approval to light the streets. In two days, the first streetlamp is lit. London has 20 miles of streets lit by gas at this time.

November 21
Two dwarfs from Santo Domingo are on view in St. Patrick's Row for 25 cents.

November 14
A pair of West African lions entertains spectators at the Horse Market.

GAS LIGHT.
PEALE'S
BALTIMORE MUSEUM
will be
ILLUMINATED
EVERY EVENING
NEAR THE THEATRE

$1200	$1150	$1100	$1050	$1000	$950	$900	$850	$800	$750	$700	$650

$1200
$1150
$1100
$1050
$1000
$950
$900
$850
$800
$750
$700
$650
$600
$550
$500
$450
$400
$350
$300
$250
$200
$150
$100
$50
$0

JAN   FEB   MAR   APR   MAY   JUN   JUL   AUG   SEP   OCT   NOV   DEC

1 8 1 7

Income $3,630.18

Income

$1200
$1150
$1100
$1050
$1000
$950
$900
$850
$800
$750
$700
$650
$600
$550
$500
$450
$400
$350
$300
$250
$200
$150
$100
$50
$0

January 28
A botanical lecture and exhibition includes a 360-ft. long painting, The Temple of Flora. *Admission is $1 at Gibney's Room on Charles Street.*

February
Gas lighting at The Peale Museum is extended from one room to all remaining galleries.

February 22
Mr. Potter, a ventriloquist and magician, performs at Butlet's Room on South Charles Street. Tickets are 75 cents.

April
The museum at Lexington and Howard Streets features 30 life-size wax figures, including fat man Daniel Lambert. A new organ plays the "Star-Spangled Banner."

French scientist Georges Cuvier proposes a new zoological classification system connecting living and fossil species for the first time.

November 27
"A certain income of $2000 a year" is promised the purchaser of the Fells Point Museum.

December 6
James West's celebrated troupe of horses appears at the Circus.

GAS LIGHT.
The Baltimore Museum
AND
Gallery of the Fine Arts,
IN HOLLIDAY-ST. NEAR THE THEATRE,
IS NOW ILLUMINATED
EVERY TUESDAY AND THURSDAY EVENINGS,
With GAS from the Company's Factory, and
is embellished with several additional
GAS CHANDELIERS.
N. B. Open as usual in the day—various late
additions.   ap 25   d4

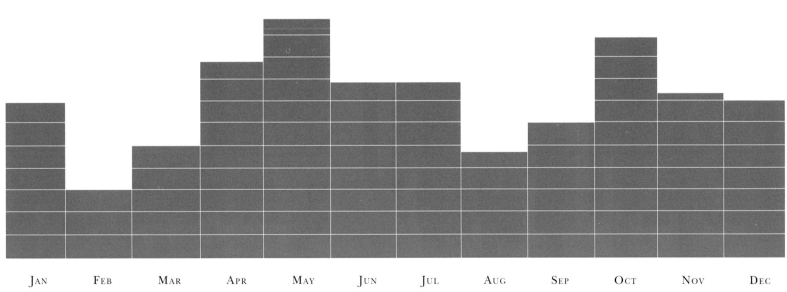

JAN   FEB   MAR   APR   MAY   JUN   JUL   AUG   SEP   OCT   NOV   DEC

1 8 1 8

Income $4,069.59

Income

$1200
$1150
$1100
$1050
$1000
$950
$900
$850
$800
$750
$700
$650
$600
$550
$500
$450
$400
$350
$300
$250
$200
$150
$100
$50
$0

January 31
A sea serpent, Scoliopnis Atlanticus, *is on view at The Peale Museum. On February 11, it moves to an exhibition room at Baltimore and Gay Streets.*

March 18–mid-April
Sena Sama, a sword-swallower from India, performs astonishing feats at the South Charles Street ballroom. Admission is $1.

March 28
The Peale Museum introduces evening chemical experiments.

Sena Sama by James Warrell

SENA SAMA
Respectfully informs the inhabitants of Baltimore that he has engaged the large *Ball Room in South Charles street,* where he will give an exhibition every evening of this week, March 16, 1818.
WONDER OF THE WORLD!!
SENA SAMA,
The Indian Juggler,
From Madras, and lately from London, and subsequently from New York, Philadelphia, &c. where he has exhibited his wonderful feats of dexterity and strength to delighted and overflowing audiences.

September 9
"Excellent kaleidoscopes" and profiles by Mr. Stillman are offered for sale at The Peale Museum.

September 12
Mr. Stanislas, direct from the Academy of Science in Paris, shows "Philosophical" and mechanical apparatus nightly at the Concert Hall on Charles Street.

October 20
The Baltimore Museum on North Howard Street displays a 21-ft. "real young sea serpent," a 14-ft. rattlesnake, the "only ostrich alive in America," and an "ouran Outang or Wild Man of the Woods."

December 11
The Vilallave family of agile acrobats performs at the Circus.

Botanist Thomas Nuttal publishes his 2-volume study, The Genera of North American Plants.

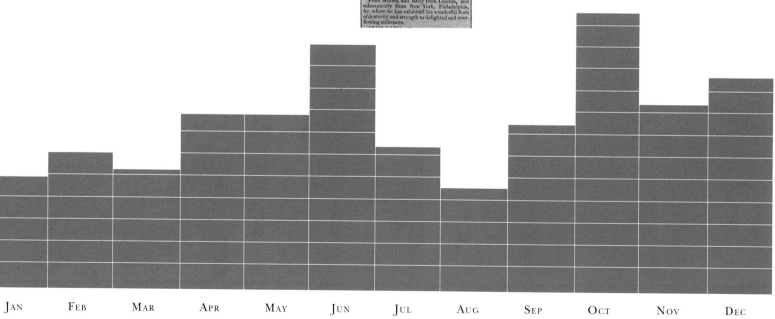

Jan   Feb   Mar   Apr   May   Jun   Jul   Aug   Sep   Oct   Nov   Dec

1819

Income $2,478.75

Income

$1200
$1150
$1100
$1050
$1000
$950
$900
$850
$800
$750
$700
$650
$600
$550
$500
$450
$400
$350
$300
$250
$200
$150
$100
$50
$0

January
Rembrandt Peale exhibits his copy of Sir Thomas Lawence's portrait of the Duke of Wellington. Retired in London after defeating Napoleon at Waterloo, the Duke frequented every popular exhibition ranging from George Catlin's American Indian paintings to the Chinese collection of a Peale Museum trustee. He also encountered Napoleon as a wax effigy at Madame Tussaud's and was "particularly amused" when the midget Tom Thumb impersonated his old enemy in 1844.

February
The exhibition of John Trumbull's painting, The Signing of the Declaration of Independence,

Gen. Andrew Jackson by Rembrandt Peale

The Duke of Wellington by Rembrandt Peale after Sir Thomas Lawrence

attracts 3,000 visitors to Baltimore's courtroom; its seven-month tour brings Trumbull over $4,000 in profits.

March 2
For one evening only, at The Peale Museum, Rembrandt Peale displays his portrait of Andrew Jackson, painted hastily when commissioned by the Baltimore City Council during the general's February 27 visit.

**May 5, 1819–
October 12, 1820**
A government expedition headed by Major Stephen H. Long explores the Louisiana Territory. Titian Peale serves as scientific artist and Thomas Say, a zoologist, identifies and names the coyote. Long's report includes the first dictionary of Plains Indian sign language.

December
An East Coast epidemic of yellow fever that killed 350 Baltimoreans and the country's financial panic account for The Peale Museum's worst year, with total income below $2,500.

The Signing of the Declaration of Independence by John Trumbull

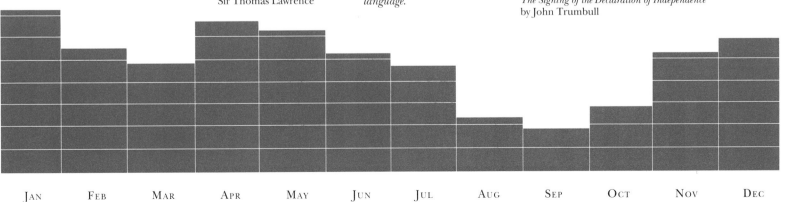

JAN   FEB   MAR   APR   MAY   JUN   JUL   AUG   SEP   OCT   NOV   DEC

1 8 2 0

Income $2,890.75

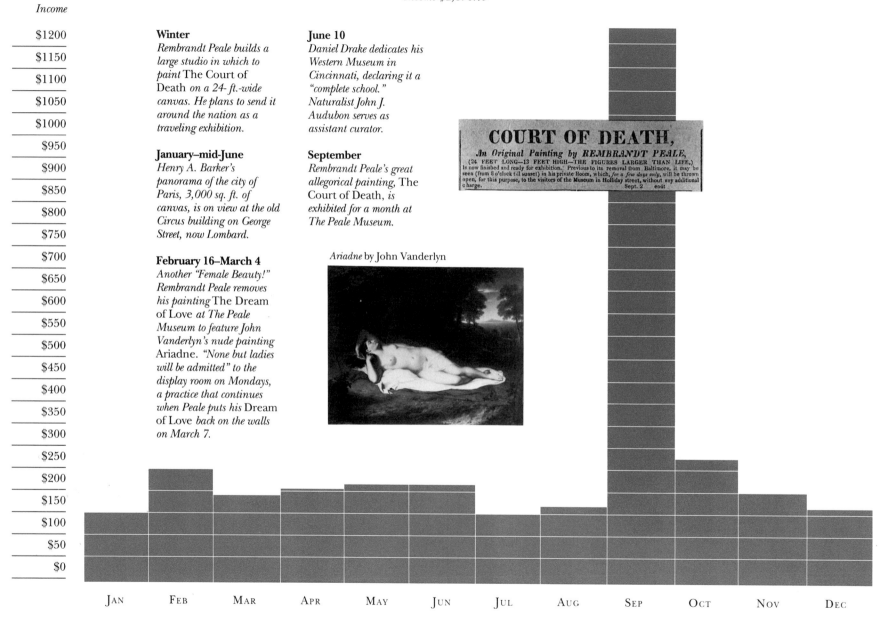

Income

$1200
$1150
$1100
$1050
$1000
$950
$900
$850
$800
$750
$700
$650
$600
$550
$500
$450
$400
$350
$300
$250
$200
$150
$100
$50
$0

Winter
Rembrandt Peale builds a large studio in which to paint The Court of Death *on a 24-ft.-wide canvas. He plans to send it around the nation as a traveling exhibition.*

January–mid-June
Henry A. Barker's panorama of the city of Paris, 3,000 sq. ft. of canvas, is on view at the old Circus building on George Street, now Lombard.

February 16–March 4
Another "Female Beauty!" Rembrandt Peale removes his painting The Dream of Love *at The Peale Museum to feature John Vanderlyn's nude painting* Ariadne. *"None but ladies will be admitted" to the display room on Mondays, a practice that continues when Peale puts his* Dream of Love *back on the walls on March 7.*

June 10
Daniel Drake dedicates his Western Museum in Cincinnati, declaring it a "complete school." Naturalist John J. Audubon serves as assistant curator.

September
Rembrandt Peale's great allegorical painting, The Court of Death, *is exhibited for a month at The Peale Museum.*

COURT OF DEATH,
An Original Painting by REMBRANDT PEALE,
(24 FEET LONG—13 FEET HIGH—THE FIGURES LARGER THAN LIFE,)
Is now finished and ready for exhibition. Previous to its removal from Baltimore, it may be seen (from 8 o'clock till sunset) in his private Room, which, *for a few days only,* will be thrown open, for this purpose, to the visitors of the Museum in Holliday street, without any additional charge.   Sept. 2   eo4t

Ariadne by John Vanderlyn

JAN   FEB   MAR   APR   MAY   JUN   JUL   AUG   SEP   OCT   NOV   DEC

I 8 2 I

Income $3,385.44

February 27
"Natural Poultry, A Cabinet of learned turkies which will dance to music" is at the Pavilion Garden. In March this remarkable show moves to Clarke's Tavern for a week.

March 26
James West's troupe at the Baltimore Circus building opens its grand spectacle of "Timour the Tartar."

April 16–June 9
Signor Hellene plays five instruments at once at The Peale Museum every evening.

April 23–mid-May
The Baltimore Theater, lit by gas, opens its season with the great English actor Edmund Kean starring in Shakespearean and other plays.

June 9
An "Esquimaux" Indian couple appears with their dog and canoe at Pavilion Garden. Tickets cost 25 cents.

October 4–late November
The Court of Death, *Rembrandt Peale's epic painting, returns to The Peale Museum.*

December 13
Haddock's "mechanical exhibition of Androids, or animated mechanism" may be seen in a room at Charles and Market Streets for 50 cents.

Income

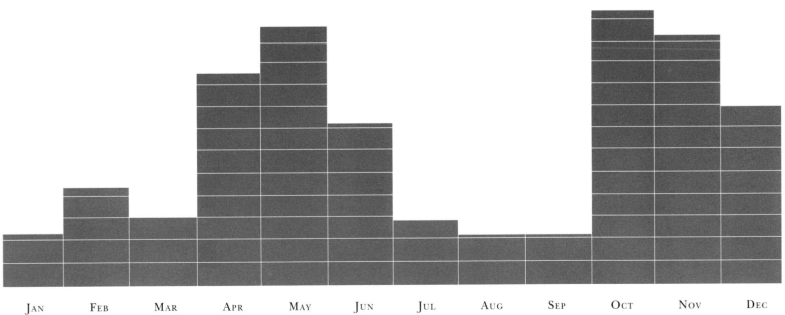

| | JAN | FEB | MAR | APR | MAY | JUN | JUL | AUG | SEP | OCT | NOV | DEC |

I 8 2 2

Income $4,196.71   Expenses $2,698.90

Income

$1200
$1150
$1100
$1050
$1000
$950
$900
$850
$800
$750
$700
$650
$600
$550
$500
$450
$400
$350
$300
$250
$200
$150
$100
$50
$0

May
Rubens Peale becomes "conductor" of The Peale Museum after brother Rembrandt's departure. He announces that the galleries will be lit every night, that new seats will be installed in the lecture gallery for scientific demonstrations, and that a band will play three evenings a week.

May 6–11
"Chinese shades," or shadow puppets, entertain at The Peale Museum.

May 17
An exhibition, "Monuments of Paris, moving by machinery," is featured at the South Charles Street Hall for 25 cents.

July 25, August 5–7, 21, 23, 24, and September 21–24
Cactus triangularis, or the rare night-blooming "Cereus," attracts huge evening crowds to The Peale Museum. The special event draws over 1,000 people on July 25 alone.

August 13
The Peale Museum inroduces live animals into its exhibits—wolves, elk, two fawns, a gray eagle, a horned owl, a red fox, a white rat, and an alligator. They are soon joined by a black bear, a ribbed-nose baboon, and a goffer turtle.

October 1
Shawishanan, a 20-year-old double-jointed Sak Indian chief only 30 inches tall and called "the greatest curiosity in America," appears at the Marsh Market. Admission is 25 cents.

October 1– November 12
Rubens Peale innaugurates The Peale Museum's first annual art exhibition, presenting 298 works.

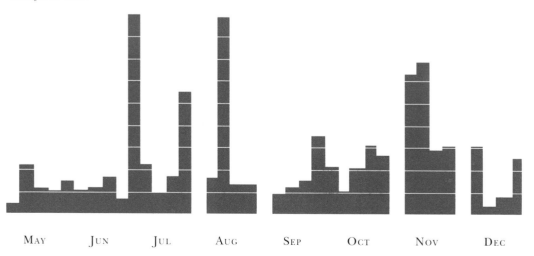

MAY   JUN   JUL   AUG   SEP   OCT   NOV   DEC

1 8 2 3

Income $4,705.75   Expenses $3,697.71

Income

$1200
$1150
$1100
$1050
$1000
$950
$900
$850
$800
$750
$700
$650
$600
$550
$500
$450
$400
$350
$300
$250
$200
$150
$100
$50
$0

January 9
The Peale Museum will demonstrate electrical experiments this evening, "provided the weather is dry."

February 26–April 9
Back from Italy, Signor Hellene performs classical music at The Peale Museum—on five instruments at once!

March 19
After travelling to Washington, a delegation of three Seneca Indian chiefs visits Baltimore and The Peale Museum, drawing crowds of onlookers during the evening who are serenaded by a band playing "Hail Columbia."

May 26
Charles Willson Peale lectures on natural history at The Peale Museum, which Rubens decorates for the occasion.

July 4
Evening holiday ticket sales at The Peale Museum total $226.

July 9
The night-blooming Cereus flowers again at The Peale Museum in the evening.

October 20– November 29
The second annual art exhibition is held at The Peale Museum.

November 11–22
Vilallave's circus features dancing on the tightrope and a Chinese performer.

Rubens Peale's expenses for March 1823

1823	Expended for the Baltimore Museum		
March			
	Gas Company	20	..
	Fuel	6	..
	Wages	23	..
	Printing	47	50
	Permanent improvements	63	35
	d°. to the house	5	87½
	Signor Hellene	160	..
	Indian Chiefs & expenses	9	95
	Miscellaneous expenses	10	51
		346	18½

CIRCUS.
Mr. VILALLAVE

JAN   FEB   MAR   APR   MAY   JUN   JUL   AUG   SEP   OCT   NOV   DEC

1 8 2 4

Income $5,854.13   Expenses $4725.75

Income

$1200
$1150
$1100
$1050
$1000
$950
$900
$850
$800
$750
$700
$650
$600
$550
$500
$450
$400
$350
$300
$250
$200
$150
$100
$50
$0

**January 23–
February 22**
*Theodore Newell
introduces his astronomi-
cal orrery to Peale
Museum visitors until
February 11. Meanwhile,
educator Joseph Lancaster
begins a lecture series on
"the moral revolution."
Rubens Peale and
Lancaster collaborate on a
book about Newell's
inventions.*

April 1–May 5
*Rembrandt Peale's
National Portrait, and
Standard Likeness of
Washington is shown at
The Peale Museum
following a January
appearance in the U.S.
Capitol.*

June 14–July 24
*Rubens Peale, "the
indefatigable proprietor of
the Museum," pays $650
for the exclusive Baltimore
exhibition of "the
Egyptian Mummy which
has excited so much
attention"—the first ever
seen in America. Along
with the mummy's
"singularly ornamented
sarcophagus, received
from ancient Thebes,"
interest is heightened by
the display of a tattooed
head from New Zealand
and G. Belzoni's
illustrated book on his
discoveries in the tombs
and temples of Egypt. In
six weeks crowds generate
an unpreceedented income
of $1,842.*

September 13
*A "transparency" of
George Washington and a
painting of the Battle of
North Point on its 10th
anniversary nets The
Peale Museum $145 in
one evening's receipts.*

The Marquis de Lafayette by
Rembrandt Peale

October 9
*Rubens Peale's account
book records that "General
Lafayette visited the
museum," resulting in an
income boost from festive
crowds of admirers.*

**October 25–
December 7**
*The Peale Museum's third
annual art exhibition
contains 300 works by the
Peale family members and
other artists.*

**December 29–
January 26, 1825**
*Henry Sargent's celebrated
painting, The Dinner
Party, is on exhibit at 173
Market Street for 25 cents;
eight months later it goes
to The Peale Museum.*

JAN   FEB   MAR   APR   MAY   JUN   JUL   AUG   SEP   OCT   NOV   DEC

I 8 2 5

Income $3,526.78   Expenses $3,196.76

Income

$1200
$1150
$1100
$1050
$1000
$950
$900
$850
$800
$750
$700
$650
$600
$550
$500
$450
$400
$350
$300
$250
$200
$150
$100
$50
$0

**January 18–
February 22**
*A "new menagerie of ten
living animals" at 72
North Howard Street
features Dandy Jack "with
feats of horsemonkeyship,
on his small Shetland
Pony."*

May
*The Peale Museum
presents "Philosophical
Fire Works" three nights a
week: a demonstration of
various gases, "aided by
machinery, producing a
great variety of colours
and forms, &c." The
Peale Museum account
book records $12 worth of
counterfeit bills taken in
during the month.*

May 16–June 30
*Rembrandt Peale's life-size
portrait of* Washington
Before Yorktown *is
exhibited at The Peale
Museum.*

July 4
*As part of their holiday
activity, Baltimoreans
crowd The Peale Museum;
evening income is $171.*

August 17
*The "Night-blooming
Cereus" that flowered at
The Peale Museum three
years ago is back with four
buds.*

September 12
*For Baltimore's annual
celebration marking the
1814 British defeat, the
front of The Peale
Museum is decorated and
a band performs. Income
for the evening is $171.*

October
*The Erie Canal links
New York City with
western New York and
the Great Lakes. Its
completion secures New
York's position as
America's commercial
center.*

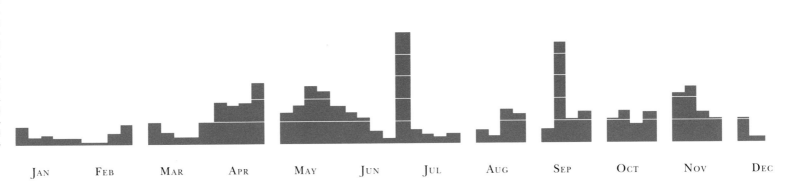

JAN   FEB   MAR   APR   MAY   JUN   JUL   AUG   SEP   OCT   NOV   DEC

1 8 2 6

Income $3,242.20 Expenses $3,168.45

Income

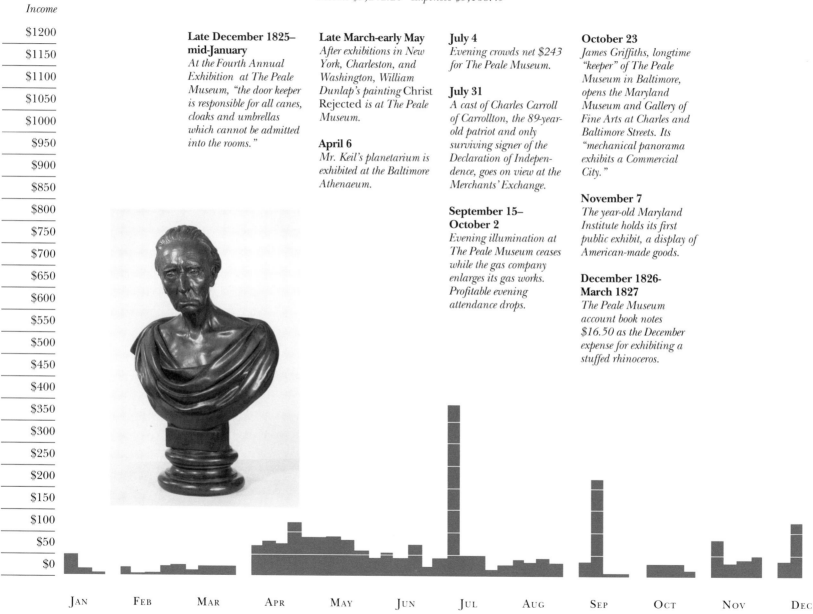

Late December 1825–mid-January
At the Fourth Annual Exhibition at The Peale Museum, "the door keeper is responsible for all canes, cloaks and umbrellas which cannot be admitted into the rooms."

Late March-early May
After exhibitions in New York, Charleston, and Washington, William Dunlap's painting Christ Rejected *is at The Peale Museum.*

April 6
Mr. Keil's planetarium is exhibited at the Baltimore Athenaeum.

July 4
Evening crowds net $243 for The Peale Museum.

July 31
A cast of Charles Carroll of Carrollton, the 89-year-old patriot and only surviving signer of the Declaration of Independence, goes on view at the Merchants' Exchange.

September 15–October 2
Evening illumination at The Peale Museum ceases while the gas company enlarges its gas works. Profitable evening attendance drops.

October 23
James Griffiths, longtime "keeper" of The Peale Museum in Baltimore, opens the Maryland Museum and Gallery of Fine Arts at Charles and Baltimore Streets. Its "mechanical panorama exhibits a Commercial City."

November 7
The year-old Maryland Institute holds its first public exhibit, a display of American-made goods.

December 1826-March 1827
The Peale Museum account book notes $16.50 as the December expense for exhibiting a stuffed rhinoceros.

I 8 2 7

Income $3,012.00   Expenses $2,907.42

Income

$1200
$1150
$1100
$1050
$1000
$950
$900
$850
$800
$750
$700
$650
$600
$550
$500
$450
$400
$350
$300
$250
$200
$150
$100
$50
$0

John James Audubon begins publishing The Birds of America *from his original drawings. A huge four-volume work, it includes prints of more than 1,000 birds. His picture of the canvasback duck includes a distant view of Baltimore.*

February 19
The Maryland Museum at Baltimore and Charles Streets adds mechanical bell-ringers and a figure of George Washington. It is gas-lit every evening and charges 25 cents for admission.

March 20
The Peale Museum boasts "many valuable additions," including a powerful electric machine "now ready for medical purposes."

April 14
Proprietor A.L. Tibbals of the Maryland Museum announces dances by five Mohawk and Seneca Indians, and pledges that the "strictest decorum and modesty will be observed throughout."

June 1
A Baltimore newspaper reveals that a mechanical "chess player is in fact a person concealed within the device." The "mechanism" is exposed, and in 1836 Edgar Allan Poe writes about the mysterious deception.

August
The popular stuffed rhino gets a second run at The Peale Museum, which pays $50 for its return.

August 12–September 15
After two months at The Peale Museum in New York, Mr. Munn presents two "learned dogs" three times daily at The Peale Museum in Baltimore. Toby tells time, answers questions, and does arithmetic. Minetto performs leaps and other tricks. A newspaper editorial commends Peale for his efforts to maintain public interest in his establishment. The five-week exhibition costs Peale $370—plus $1 to clean the lecture room—against income of $1,105.

JAN   FEB   MAR   APR   MAY   JUN   JUL   AUG   SEP   OCT   NOV   DEC

1 8 2 8

Income $3,080.22   Expenses $2,362.97

February 18–27
Mr. E. Reynolds performs on the "Irish Union Pipes" at The Peale Museum.

Mid-February–mid-March
Onondaga Indians perform six dances daily at The Peale Museum, an expense of $272.60.

April 3–May 17
The appearance of Mr. Hannington and his trained dog, Apollo, costs The Peale Museum $315.12. On May 2, Apollo's tricks are applauded by 70 admiring ladies.

May 5–June 17
The "First Annual Exhibition" of art is held in the Maryland Museum at Baltimore and Charles Streets.

May 29–June 1
Models of railroad engines, wagons, and tracks are exhibited at the Merchant's Exchange.

July 4
The Peale Museum displays paintings of Charles Carroll and the new railroad.

August 31–early January 1829
At the New Rotunda, Calvert and Pleasant Streets, a panorama of Niagara Falls is lit at night by more than 200 gas lamps. Admission is 25 cents.

September 3–24
"The Old Favorite Returned," the learned dog Apollo returns to The Peale Museum. His success attracts rival dog Don Carlo to Baltimore for a month beginning in mid-September.

November 3–February 22, 1829
Miss Honeywell is engaged for $30 a week to appear at The Peale Museum in Baltimore after nearly three months at The Peale Museum in New York. Born without arms, she cuts paper, writes, draws, and sews, using her mouth and feet.

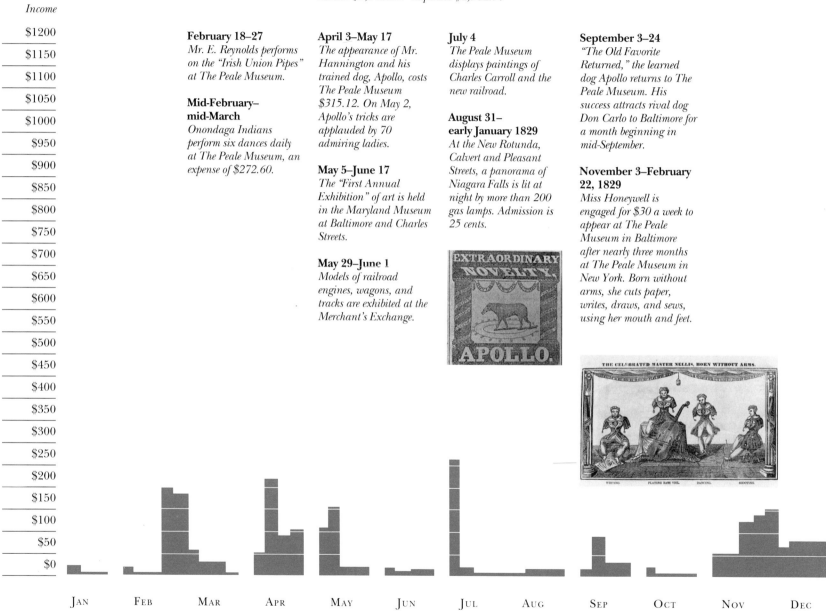

Income

$1200
$1150
$1100
$1050
$1000
$950
$900
$850
$800
$750
$700
$650
$600
$550
$500
$450
$400
$350
$300
$250
$200
$150
$100
$50
$0

JAN   FEB   MAR   APR   MAY   JUN   JUL   AUG   SEP   OCT   NOV   DEC

1 8 2 9

Income $1,480.35 Expenses $1,412.89

Income

$1200
$1150
$1100
$1050
$1000
$950
$900
$850
$800
$750
$700
$650
$600
$550
$500
$450
$400
$350
$300
$250
$200
$150
$100
$50
$0

February 4–7
Traveling to Washington, famed Indian chief Red Jacket speaks at The Peale Museum, with translations by Captain Johnson.

Early March
Between appearances at The Peale Museum in New York, four Sandusky Indians appear at The Peale Museum in Baltimore for two weekss, and then move to the rival Maryland Museum for a month to perform their dances and the "maneuvers of scalping."

March 14–28
An Egyptian mummy fascinates crowds during its display at The Peale Museum.

April 2–23
Paintings of King George IV and the Destruction of Sodom are on display at The Peale Museum.

May 15
Fourteen paintings of actors and actresses are for sale at The Peale Museum. Unsold, they are moved in 1853 to the Towson home of actor John Owens, a later owner of the museum.

June 9
At the Baltimore Atheneum is Rand's improved solar microscope, exhibited in Boston and New York City, "Magnifying 400,000 of times." Admission is only 50 cents on sunny days.

July 16–August 25
Puppets Punch and Judy perform twice daily for "the small fry crowd in the exhibition room" of The Peale Museum.

September 10– November 18
Former London museum operator William Bullock's 3,000-sq.-ft. panorama of Mexico City, painted by Robert Burford, is displayed at the Rotunda on North Calvert Street.

September 12
The new Washington Museum in Baltimore opens. Proprietors William Crouch (once Rubens Peale's assistant) and John P. Paul advertise a 22-ft. boa constrictor.

September 24
Baltimore's first public primary school opens. Within two months, there are four, two for boys and two for girls.

October 29
The armless silhouette artist, Miss Honeywell, is now working at 112 Baltimore Street.

December 5
The Peale Museum in Baltimore closes its doors on Holliday Street and moves to a rented building at Baltimore and Calvert Streets that opens January 1, 1830. Sold for $1,610 and remodeled in 1830, the original museum building becomes Baltimore's first City Hall.

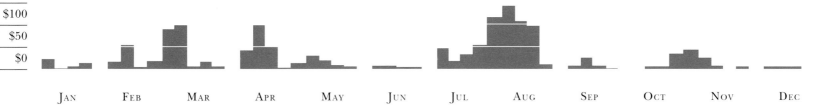

JAN   FEB   MAR   APR   MAY   JUN   JUL   AUG   SEP   OCT   NOV   DEC

Designed & Published by W. Birch Enamel Painter 1800.

Peale's Museum:
Politics, Idealism, and Public Patronage
in the Early Republic

Ruth Helm

At the time William Birch published this engraving, Charles Willson Peale operated his museum in Philosophical Hall, seen here through the trees. In 1802, with the popularity of the mastodon exhibition, the museum expanded into the upper floors of the State House. Visitors paid 25 cents to see the displays in the State House, and another 50 cents to see the mastodon and exhibits in Philosophical Hall.

In 1786, Charles Willson Peale began a new and ambitious project. An energetic painter of some renown, he had established an art gallery in his Philadelphia home, "ornamenting" the exhibition room with his own portraits of "distinguished characters in the revolutionary-war."[1] On the eve of the Philadelphia Convention, however, a new sense of expectant optimism gripped the United States, and the vast potential of the new nation excited schemes of future glory. While Benjamin Rush confidently declared that "we have only finished the first act of the great drama," and predicted the imminent rise of a noble and enlightened nation,[2] Peale easily caught the expansive spirit of the age. If Rush and others envisioned a system of schools and colleges in every state capped by a distinguished national university, Peale clearly understood the limited prospects of merely developing a private portrait gallery. Thus, he announced in the *Pennsylvania Packet* his intention to expand his art gallery to include "a Repository for Natural curiosities" and "Wonderful Works of Nature," each "classed," "arranged," and identified according to "the place from whence it came." At first Peale expected the new museum simply to "please and entertain the Public," but by 1790 he proposed "to encrease the Museum to a national Magnitude," and by 1792 he aspired to nothing less than achieving an international reputation and world fame. "The plan is now laid," Peale wrote to Tobias Lear, "to produce a Depository of subjects in natural history" which would quickly become the equal of any museum in Europe.[3]

Although Peale initially solicited "Assistance in this Undertaking" from individual citizens, his sense of the museum's increasing importance and its presumed association with the projected national university, necessitated another form of patronage. A museum intended to educate the citizens of the republic,[4] to inspire national pride by acquainting the larger world with American specimens, and eventually to signal the acceptance of American naturalists into the international scientific community required, in Peale's view, the financial support and legal protection of the government.

Charles Willson Peale informed Americans in 1790 that every great national museum in the world had begun as a private collection.

Third and Lombard
By Rubens Peale, 1858–1860
American Philosophical Society, Philadelphia

Charles Willson Peale's museum began in his home at the corner of Third and Lombard Streets in Philadelphia in 1784. Ten years later he moved the museum to Philosophical Hall near the Pennsylvania State House.

He often commented that the great British Museum had been founded after physician and botanist Sir Hans Sloane bequeathed his vast collections to the nation. Peale may also have known that when the Prince of Wales viewed Sloane's accumulated treasures just before the collector's death, he reportedly expressed "the great pleasure it gave him to see so magnificent a collection in *England*."[5] If an enlightened nobleman could pronounce Sloane's collecting efforts "an ornament" to England that "must conduce to the benefit of learning," then Peale believed he had a justifiable and parallel claim in his own country. And if the Prince acknowledged "how great an honour will redound to *Britain*, to have [Sloane's collection] established for publick use to the latest posterity," Peale drew on respected and aristocratic opinion in insisting that his own museum must also evolve into a flourishing institution belonging to "the great Public of the American States."[6] A republican nation, however, dependent upon an enlightened citizenry, had an even more compelling reason to found a great public museum; in 1807 Peale observed that great projects that will ultimately benefit the United States should certainly enjoy legislative support. Although begun as private enterprises, such things as canals, roads, and museums, that are "for a public benefit," according to Peale, "should be a public charge."[7]

Developing an approach founded on republican principles as well as tradition, Peale continued to encourage public funding for the development of his own contribution to the public good. Writing to the newly elected James Madison in 1809, he reviewed the arguments for nationalization of his museum and its removal to the city of Washington; the museum's proven usefulness and importance; the approbation of American and foreign "scientific men"; the lack of adequate space to display newly acquired articles in its present location; his own fears that the collection "might be scattered and lost to the public" in the event of his death; new exhibits of "American Manufactures" which do "our Country credit"; the wide array of raw materials acquainting citizens with the nation's natural resources. With such a concentration of useful objectives, Peale repeated his claim of the museum's value as a popular educational institution, concluding that "in a Political view how immencely important an extended Museum might be rendered." Then "would it not be an important Establishment at the seat of Government?" Peale asked Madison. Even the loss of 6 percent interest that the museum presently produced in Philadelphia would be offset since "the influence of Public men" would undoubtedly encourage an increase of valuable donations. Moreover, Peale assured Madison of his own unselfish, republican motives, declaring that the topic of public support for the museum seemed "important to my Country," and "if properly managed, it is undoubtedly so."[8]

In this same spirit, Peale had already approached President George Washington. He had known Washington during the war, was "grateful for past favors," and had no wish to be "troublesome." Yet the lack of local portrait commissions in Philadelphia during the 1790s forced him to "make journeys into Maryland to seek employment," thus preventing him from developing the "public benefit" of the museum. In order to remain in Philadelphia "near Congress, and [to place] my Museum under their Patronage" while gaining time to expand the scope of the collection, Peale asked Washington for an appointment to the vacant office of postmaster general.[9] Washington, who had contributed several golden pheasants to Peale for preservation and display and would privately purchase four annual admissions in 1795, had no inclination to offer public support either to the museum or the museum-keeper.

Undeterred, in 1801 Peale again inquired of Secretary of State James Madison "whether any and what expectation may be indulged of the Museum ever being taken over under Public patronage."[10] This idea had been his "grand *Ultimation,*" he confessed, assuring Madison "that a vast deal may be done in a permanent way with but a trifling expence" to the nation. The following year, citing the "public utility" of the museum to "enlighten" his countrymen, "humanize the minds, promote harmony, and aid Virtue," Peale asked President Thomas Jefferson whether the United States government would "give an encouragement and make provision for the Establishment of this Museum in the City of Washington."[11] Peale acknowledged that the raw, new capital city would draw few visitors to a museum, yet from his point of view, with government subsidies sufficiently generous "to make up such deficiencies," donations would "naturally flow in" and "amply repay the expence."

Washington and Jefferson, who approved of both science and museums and endorsed the idea of a national university, nevertheless had reservations about Peale's request for public funds. Although Peale's idea had cur-

rency, and learned societies as well as various schemes to educate the general population proliferated in the Early Republic, none of these enterprises received direct financial support from the government. Washington believed that Peale's museum was a private concern and should remain privately funded,[12] and Jefferson informed Peale in 1802 "that one of the great questions which had divided political opinion in this country is whether Congress are authorised by the constitution to apply the public money to any but the purposes specially enumerated in the Constitution."[13]

Apart from the question of legality, however, the changing social structure of the Congress was enough to make public funding doubtful. According to some observers in the 1780s, "Specious, interested, designing men," "men, respectable neither for their property, their virtue, nor their abilities," "men without reading, experience, or principle" had come into power, putting government "into the Hands of those whose ability or situation in Life does not intitle them to it"[14] and who would, in any case, not be disposed to voting public money for a natural history museum. But whether those congressmen were philistines or merely thrifty, ordinary citizens who increasingly won elections, Peale acknowledged a decided lack of interest in the legislature for his proposals. By 1819, after three exasperating decades of trying to nationalize the museum, Peale doubted whether "the majority of the Legislature are sufficiently illuminated to appreciate"[15] its merits or importance.

Charles Willson Peale's arguments for nationalization—consistently employed until

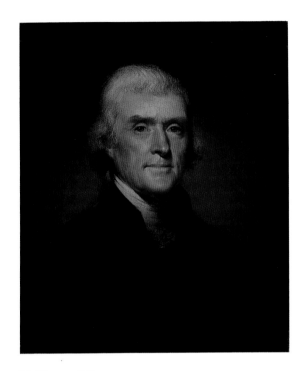

1819—never succeeded in convincing Congress of the propriety or necessity of the expense. Disappointed and often deeply pained, Peale believed "that the time will come when they shall be sorry for having let it slip through their fingers." "The education it is capable of diffusing through the mass of Citizens," he wrote to Jefferson, "is all important."[16] At the close of both their lives, however, the best comfort Jefferson could offer Peale was to suggest that the museum "will immortalise your name," and then to recommend that "your body must be deposited in its center, under a Mausoleum, light and tasty."[17]

Peale regularly contended for federal subsidies, but he simultaneously sought alternate sources of public financing. Even before approaching the United States government, and despite his ambitions to establish a truly national institution, Peale had turned with equal earnestness to the State of Pennsylvania. Given the impediments of presidential doubts and congressional reluctance, Jefferson thought this approach had merit, remarking in 1802 that "the legislature of your own state furnishes at present the best prospect."[18]

Since 1792, however, Peale had been requesting "pecuniary aid" from the Pennsylvania Assembly to improve the museum,[19] and in 1794 had made another appeal for a low-interest loan to expand the facility. Irritated with the recalcitrance of the Assembly, Peale added a measure of determination to the familiar argument of the museum's usefulness to the public. Even though it pained him that his "friends in the House of Assembly should have so much trouble in the passage of my Bill," Peale nevertheless assured his allies in

the Pennsylvania Legislature that he intended, now that hope of funding had "vanished," to "prove" the great "advantage to the Public generally, and the State in Particular" of Peale's museum.[20] By 1795, however, Peale had proved nothing, and had not ceased complaining that "The Government has not yet done anything for me." Although the museum had slowly improved, he objected nevertheless that "it is like roling a heavy stone up a steep sandy hill, having no funds to support it but of my own earning."[21]

In the election year of 1800, amid the heated contest that ended the glittering Federalist era and swept the more egalitarian Jeffersonians to power, Peale tried once more to convince the assembly of the "urgency" of providing public assistance. Expressing his hope to Timothy Matlack that the museum "shall open a road" for the future promotion of republicanism, and protesting again an insufficiency of adequate exhibition space, Peale requested that the legislature, then sitting at Lancaster, "appropriate" the old State House at Philadelphia for the use of the museum.[22] Appealing once more to national pride, he argued that his museum could someday surpass any British institution of natural history, and that the French, whose own revolution the Jeffersonians continued to admire, "have not spared expence to promote this Service."[23] Peale asked only for use of a public building no longer serving its original purpose. This happy arrangement, he assured Governor Thomas McKean, would allow him to apply more of his own funds to "an Institution which now ought to be considered as a public School of Information to multitudes of every Class of citizens."[24]

Although the Pennsylvania Legislature failed to act on Peale's petition in 1800,[25] and he threatened "to obtain aid from some other of the United States,"[26] only his famous excavation of the mastodon skeleton in 1801 and the popularity of its exhibition at the museum, gave his request to remove from Philosophical Hall to the State House a new and attractive immediacy. Peale even proposed a new museum building, designed by Benjamin Henry Latrobe, to be constructed in the State House Yard and financed by a State-approved lottery.[27] Although Peale's son Rembrandt, as we shall see, will construct in 1814 the first building specifically planned and designed as a museum, the prospect of the destruction of the State House garden by new construction alarmed Philadelphians at the turn of the century, and moved the City Councils and the Philosophical Society to intervene; each of these bodies suggested that the Assembly grant partial use of the existing State House to Peale, leaving the Yard and gardens for public enjoyment.[28]

Pleased by the turn of events, Peale lobbied on his own behalf, expressing the familiar hope that "the honor of republicanism" would drive the Legislature to approve the measure. He pointed out again that larger quarters would improve the museum's development and facilitate its republican mission, giving it such prominence and credibility "as will illuminate the Sons of Pennsyl[a] to her most distant bounds of Territory."[29]

Responding perhaps to pressure from the influential membership of the City Councils and the Philosophical Society, the Pennsylvania Assembly allowed the upper story of the State House, and the lower east room (where the Declaration of Independence had been signed) for the use of Peale's museum.[30] Much "gratified" by this legislative action, Peale prepared to convince those who had opposed the bill of the museum's utility and importance. In his view, even hostile congressmen, "when they find [the museum's] tendency to promote Virtue and morality," will happily provide public patronage for its future support.[31]

Yet Peale occupied these quarters only "at the pleasure" of the Pennsylvania Legislature, whose more commercial-minded and frugal members in 1811 defeated a new resolution allowing the museum to remain permanently in the State House.[32] Peale remarked that even though "many of the Members are very friendly to me, and desirous to give the building for the use of the Museum," it pained him nevertheless that "there are many no doubt who will endeavor to Have the whole [State House] square sold."[33] The following year, Peale rather testily refused to approach the new Assembly, explaining to Governor Snyder that the museum presently enjoyed wide public acclaim—earned by his own great and prolonged labors—and it was now the Assembly's obligation "to make provision for securing it to the public."[34]

Throughout the years that Peale guided the affairs of the museum, he consistently and repeatedly proclaimed the financial advantages of political patronage. Writing to Charles Biddle in 1812, he articulated once again his fundamental argument for government assistance. Although Peale could "scarcely believe" the Pennsylvania Legislature's continued failure to install the museum permanently in the State House, he often pointed out that his proposals cost the State nothing.[35] In fact, with firm and committed government support, the small admission fee paid by numerous citizen-visitors and the certain flood of donated objects from an admiring public, would allow the museum both to fulfill its republican purpose and to flourish as a self-supporting institution.

To his constant chagrin, however, Peale's views rarely coincided with those of the men who dispensed public money. In 1816 the City of Philadelphia purchased the State House from the State, plunging the museum into a new "crisis," according to Peale, by demanding that he rent the quarters occupied by the museum.[36] Required to pay a "most exorbitant" amount of $1,600 per year, carry insurance on the building, keep the steeple clock in good repair, and ring the great bell to warn of fires,[37] Peale now had to confront the civic government on the issue of patronage, refusing once again to yield the museum's status as a public benefit or concede the appropriateness of government support.

Peale first addressed a plea to "the more enlightened" citizens of Philadelphia, finding a sympathetic group willing to petition the Councils on his behalf. Peale and his supporters, however, faced increasingly entrenched opposition. The Select and Common Councils proved hostile to arguments for patronage, resenting interference in their deliberative affairs and taking no action whatsoever. Even some irritated private citizens took exception to Peale's demands and assumptions.[38] Still Peale persisted, gathering his forces and proposing a new plan of his own devising to the Councils in 1817. Insisting as always that the museum was "not only honorable but advanta-

geous" to Philadelphia, and perfectly "calculated to diffuse a taste for rational and moral recreation" in the Republic, he offered to deliver to the City "right and title" to the museum forever, pay $800 per year in rent, provide an annual appropriation of $400 for internal improvements, and maintain the collection. In return Peale expected guaranteed tenancy in the State House, control of museum revenues above the amount stipulated for the City, and continued management of the museum by the Peale family.[39]

Privately, however, Peale despaired of success, expressing his "belief that the Corporation will not accede to my proposition" even though his proposal allowed the City to "reap all the benefit of such an Establishment without a single cent expence."[40] In his view, the present problem centered on a conspiracy against him, "a combination of attorneys" on the committee investigating the plan, men who resorted to "chicanery" and deception to prevent its enactment by the Councils.[41] A "number of Attornies at Law," he told Jefferson, "are desirous to get the rooms we occupy" in the State House for themselves, and will undoubtedly "swerve the Councils from their duty."[42]

Whether Peale correctly assessed the situation or not, the committee recommended against his proposal in January 1818. Citing the danger from Peale's recent installation of gas lights and the cost of fire insurance, Peale's failure to convince them of the necessity of his demands, and his own admission that "the number of visitors to the Museum continues to be as great as heretofore," the committee proposed that the Councils reject Peale's "terms and conditions," fix the rent at

$1,200 per annum, and prohibit Peale from manufacturing gas for the use of lighting on the premises.[43]

Peale responded to the news with his usual lament over the loss of "a valuable Institution to the City," and considered offering the museum to the United States Congress as a means of motivating Philadelphia to "embrace my proposition."[44] In 1820, he again petitioned the City Councils to reduce his rent, asserting that he could not "doubt [their] willingness to promote the usefulness of the Museum."[45]

But government patronage eluded Peale until the end of his life. As late as 1824 he blamed the trustees of the Philadelphia Museum Company, who should "have been more active to obtain aid from the [City] Corporation," while he himself renewed the endless wait "to meet with the encouragement which such an Institution deserves."[46] Moreover, "My labours in forming this establishment," he unhappily observed, are more esteemed "by foreigners than by my Countrymen and all strangers cry out shame, when they hear that I pay a high rent for part of the State house occupied by the Museum." From his expectations of founding a great national museum under the aegis of the United States to haggling with the City Corporation over rent, Charles Willson Peale's arguments for public patronage and his beleaguered sense of disappointment remained consistent.

Apart from blaming the ignoble insensitivity of Congress and the ineptitude of his managers, Peale had other explanations for the museum's failure to receive public funding. Assuredly, his argument for support was itself obsolete, bound by traditional assumptions in a rapidly changing world. While Peale insisted that the museum would admirably serve republicanism by educating the population, inspiring morality, and encouraging a selfless devotion to the state, the nation turned increasingly toward commerce and individualism. Even the scientific rationalism so well expressed in the Linnaean arrangements of his exhibits, jarred uncomfortably with the rising mystical currents of the Second Great Awakening.[47]

Yet Peale seems not to have acknowledged the passing of the old republican ideals, alluding instead to certain petty jealousies and misunderstandings over his personal profits that caused the Legislature to deny him government support. Since the public benefit from the museum exceeded the amount of the government's patronage, "It is not necessary," he observed to Governor Snyder, "for narrow-minded persons to calculate the advantages" he personally derived from the museum.[48] Moreover, the Committee of the Councils had demanded an exorbitant rent for the State House simply because they believed erroneously that he "was making an immence fortune by the Museum."[49] "Reflect," he wrote to Rembrandt as his son prepared to follow the family tradition by starting a new museum of his own in Baltimore, "how much I have done to make a Museum which is a public advantage, and see how much I am envied the small advantages I receive from the State of Pennsylvania."[50]

Charles Willson Peale had often solicited government favors for Rembrandt as well as for himself, requesting on his son's behalf such perquisites as a federal clerkship, presidential sittings for portraits, and congressional approval of money bills for the purchase of Rembrandt's paintings.[51] These instances of support, however, concerned his son's career as an artist and not a museumkeeper, and although Peale continually encouraged Rembrandt to excel in "the art," promoting him as the foremost painter in America and proudly pointing out his accomplishments, he argued vehemently against the foundation of the Baltimore museum.

By 1812, Rembrandt Peale had been deeply wounded by certain allegations against his artistic integrity. The young painter had been accused of plagiarism,[52] and although he successfully and defiantly defended his professional honor, the affront left him bitter and alienated. Rather than risk further humiliation in Philadelphia where he had opened a studio and gallery, and anticipating lingering defamatory innuendoes, Rembrandt Peale proposed abandoning painting and inaugurating the new Baltimore museum.[53]

His father, however, strongly advised against the plan, suggesting that it was misguided, ill-conceived, and doomed to certain failure.[54] Ignorant of the "trouble and expense of a Museum" and the unreliability of prospective investors "when it comes to touch their cash," Peale insisted that Rembrandt was unprepared to cope with the "vexations" of the Baltimore venture. He would, moreover, embarrass his sister Angelica and her aristocratic husband, a Baltimorean who regarded museums as squalid centers of low entertainment rather than "temples of wisdom." Among other things, Peale also contended that Rembrandt paid insufficient attention to "Classical arrangement" of objects, and even worse, he foolishly ignored the financial burden of assuming a heavy debt. "Avoid debt as you would strong drink," Peale advised, remember that "Interest of money" drives all men, and if you borrow "Pay day will come." Rembrandt, according to Charles Willson Peale, who had spent twenty-six years in building a museum, should resolutely apply himself to painting and put aside his injured feelings.

Although Peale's embroilment over patronage with the Legislature of Pennsylvania and the Councils of Philadelphia occurred simultaneously with Rembrandt's proposal, he made no mention of the difficulty of obtaining public funds in his wide-ranging and pointed objections to Rembrandt's scheme. Peale assured Nathaniel Ramsay that he had used every conceivable argument, had "touched every string that I thought would vibrate" to discourage Rembrandt from undertaking the project,[55] yet he did not include the troublesome lack of government support. Thus, from its inception, Rembrandt Peale's Baltimore museum seems to have been a private, commercial enterprise—a profit-making institution founded to enrich the proprietor rather than educate the public. Rembrandt, his father observed, having foolishly abandoned painting for a living, now "believes . . . he can best support himself and his large and increasing family" by establishing a museum of his own, but the undertaking, he warned, "will require an uncommon industry" to produce financial independence.[56] Whereas Peale had long declared that the government was obliged to provide adequate and permanent quarters for the Philadelphia museum, Rembrandt hired an architect and solicited subscriptions to pay for construction of a museum building in Baltimore. And while

Peale had asked whether "we [can] expect in any of our Cities sufficient means from the Government to Establish a Classical arranged collection of Subjects of Nature and art in a sufficient Building?"[57] Rembrandt amassed a construction debt of $14,000. "Ought not the City," Peale had wondered, "provide a good [museum] building . . . for the improvement of its Citizens?" while Rembrandt established a privately funded "Elegant Rendezvous for taste, curiosity and leisure."[58] As Rembrandt explained to Jefferson, he intended "to form a handsome establishment" in Baltimore, including an art gallery, a "Repository of the course and products of manufactures," and some natural history exhibits.[59] He had no plans, however, to recall the republican mission of the Philadelphia museum, but rather to appeal to "Ladies as Arbiters of Fashion" and gentlemen of taste who would find Peale's Baltimore museum a "fashionable lounge" and a "popular place of evening resort."[60] This museum, Rembrandt assured Jefferson "will differ from my father's" and represent a new age and decidedly different values.

For this reason alone, Charles Willson Peale may have initially discouraged Rembrandt from establishing the Baltimore museum. Although entertainments had been offered at Philadelphia at the suggestion of his other sons, he had accepted them uncomfortably as practical, if offensive, measures to increase visitation. As a member of the Revolutionary generation and a strong believer in the ideological principles of the era, Peale surely proved disappointed with his son's approach. Thus, the two museums, existing simultaneously, signaled a jarring discontinu-

ity. Moreover, Peale had already selected and approved Rembrandt's profession, judging him a gifted painter destined for greatness and the glorification of the family name through art. He had himself retired from painting in 1794 in order to devote himself fully to his museum, explicitly designating Rembrandt (and his oldest son Raphaelle) as his successors in the portrait business. Charles Willson Peale, who had clearly intended to direct Rembrandt's future, therefore viewed the Baltimore venture as an unfortunate assertion of filial independence.[61] But more important than the loss of parental authority or the rejection of republican values, was the threat to Peale's self-appointed position in American society. Rembrandt, whom Peale acknowledged had talents "superior in many respects" to his own,[62] challenged his father's attempts to become the most eminent museum-keeper in the nation.

Peale had expressed great confidence at the founding of his museum, firmly declaring in 1786 that if he lived long enough his "labours will make a museum that will be considered of more consequence than any thing of this sort in America."[63] And if he complained in 1813 that Rembrandt had become a rival who thinks "he can form a Museum far exceeding what I have done"[64] and argued strenuously against his son's proposal, perhaps at that moment Peale feared the success of the Baltimore museum more than its failure. His own troubled attempts to convince federal and local legislatures of the need for museums and the necessity of sustaining them with public funds, seems to have had no noticeable bearing on his objections in this uniquely complex and emotional matter.

Yet Charles Willson Peale continued to prod the government until the end of his life, believing that museums served a national purpose and filled a national need. He would have sold his collection to the nation, the state, or the city for a handsome sum, or donated it in return for financial security. Barring those events, however, he would gladly have accepted patronage in any form. Apart from his prolonged efforts on behalf of the Philadelphia museum, and despite his seeming reluctance to approach Congress for Rembrandt's benefit, in 1822 Peale wrote to Secretary of War John C. Calhoun on a related matter with familiar resonances:

> My Son Rubens is desirous to know what encouragement might be obtained to establish a Museum in the City of Washington, provided this undertaking was qualified to render it a scientific and well organized Institution for diffusing general knowledge.

Peale explicitly wished to know "whether a building would be given that would be sufficiently large to make a beginning . . . ."[65]

By mid-century a beginning had indeed been made and a building given, but the new national "Museum in the City of Washington," the "scientific and well organized institution for diffusing general knowledge" that emerged in the 1840s, reaffirmed the opposition to public support that had always thwarted the best efforts of Charles Willson Peale.

In 1826, the year before Peale died at Philadelphia, James Smithson arranged to bequeath his large fortune to the United States of America. An English aristocrat and devoted scientist, Smithson directed the American government, upon his death and on the condition that his only heir died childless, to establish in his name an institution "for the increase & diffusion of Knowledge among men." Thus Congress, uncertain of the proper disposition of private funds for public use, often immobilized, and still displaying its traditional lack of enthusiasm for schemes that increased or diffused public knowledge, finally authorized the foundation of the Smithsonian Institution in 1846. But if the architect James Renwick, Jr. designed a "cathedral to science" to house the nation's official scientific institution, and if the Smithsonian promoted the cause of American scientific discovery as well as the education of the public, it did so without the use of public funds. Only the resources of a private donor would make Charles Willson Peale's great dream a reality. ❖ ❖ ❖

Social Class and Participation at Peale's Philadelphia Museum

David R. Brigham

The Artist in his Museum (left)
Self-portrait by Charles Willson Peale, 1822
Pennsylvania Academy of Fine Arts
Gift of Mrs. Sarah Harrison (The Joseph Harrison, Jr. Collection)

Charles Willson Peale's career as painter, naturalist, and museum visionary is brilliantly delineated in this autobiographical portrait painted at the age of 81. The painting reveals not only the importance of the mastodon and other works of nature, but also the awe and contemplation he hoped to inspire in the museum's visitors.

In Europe, all men of information prize a well regulated museum, as a necessary appendage to government, but in several parts of that quarter of the earth, the means of visiting those repositories, are within the reach of particular classes of society only, or open on such terms or at such portions of time, as effectually to debar the mass of society, from participating in the improvement, and the pleasure resulting from a careful visitation.

Both Charles Willson Peale writing on his own behalf, as quoted above, and current scholars maintain that Peale's museum was accessible to both the elite and popular members of American society.[1] Advertisements for the museum suggest an intended audience by demonstrating that Peale shared conventional language of promotion with institutions of learning and leisure. Subscribers to annual tickets of admission to the museum enumerate an actual patron base, from which the socio-economic status of Peale's patrons may be determined. Was Peale's museum open on equal terms to constituents with diverse class affiliations?

Contemporary discussions about education often depended upon the concept of "useful knowledge," a principle to which Peale subscribed. Only when subsequent application of the knowledge gained was anticipated or demonstrated was the time spent deemed to have been justified. Pursuits of useless knowledge constituted lost social utility, since these efforts disqualified their participants from "active pursuits in life." According to this anonymous author, the wealthy were most often guilty of this social transgression, since only they could afford to engage in such "trifling studies." Discussions of the moral import of education often contrasted a life of application and industry with one of excessive leisure, and identified youth as the age to begin on the proper path. Commitment to useful knowledge guaranteed a long and satisfying life, one author proposed, while slothfulness in youth led to an empty, bitter boredom in old age. As a man who returned from retirement to manage the museum at age 81, who proceeded to paint the most ambitious self-portrait (page 78) of his career later that year, and who continued to work at such inventions as improved porcelain false teeth into the last days of his nearly 86 year life, Peale surely counted himself among the moral exemplars of this author's model. Peale's commitment to the concept of "useful knowledge" was institutionalized in the 17 year (1794-1811) residence of his family and the museum at the Hall of the American Philosophical Society for Promoting Useful Knowledge.[2]

Peale's institutional affiliations helped to legitimize his promotion of the museum as educationally serious. Peale's election to the American Philosophical Society in 1786, following two weeks after the museum's opening announcement, began a relationship that publicly linked Peale to Philadelphia's learned community. Eighteen months later, Peale was elected one of three curators of the society, an office he shared until 1811 with University of Pennsylvania professors Benjamin Smith Barton, Robert Patterson, and Robert Hare, Jr., Swedish Church minister Nicholas Collin, Pennsylvania Hospital physician Thomas Parke, inventor Robert Leslie, and others. This demonstrates the breadth of educated peers whom Peale encountered as a member and an officer. Among other duties, curators maintained the society's library and their cabinet of mechanical models, fossil bones, minerals, and other items of scientific and historical significance. Pierre Eugene Du Simitiere, the first private museum operator in Philadelphia, preceded Peale in the society with election to membership in 1768 and to curator in 1776, 1779, and 1781. Both the cabinet of the society and Du Simitiere's American Museum were among the models of collecting, organization, and display upon which Peale built his Philadelphia Museum. In 1794 Peale moved the museum from the domestic space of his home on Lombard Street (page 68) to the center of government and learning in Philosophical Hall (page 66), among the buildings of the State House complex.[3]

Peale replaced the outgoing University of Pennsylvania as a tenant in Philosophical Hall, another educational institution to which Peale attached his reputation. When Peale began his lecture series later in the decade, he did so each season "in the Hall of the University." This entrance into the city's most prestigious place of learning established a tone of academic seriousness for the lectures. In turn, Charles Caldwell affirmed the merit of Peale's collections when he announced to his university students in natural history that "the classical and demonstrative part of the course will be delivered in Mr. Peale's Museum."[4]

Peale established less formal connections with the University of Pennsylvania by enlisting its professors in the development of the museum. Peale's audience was occasionally reminded that mathematics professor Robert Patterson donated the first natural history specimen, a paddle fish, to the museum. In lectures and then in his self-portrait Peale reminded the public of Patterson's role: "With this article, the/Museum commenced/ June 1784./Pres. by M:[r] R Patterson." In forming a Committee of Visitors and Directors of the Museum in 1792, an advisory board that Peale hoped would bolster his chances for public funding, he again included university professors: Benjamin Smith Barton, Robert Patterson, David Rittenhouse, and Caspar Wistar.[5]

Peale's relationship to the Library Company of Philadelphia, another carefully honed

1813
Massachusetts Historical Society

This six-month admissions pass to the Philadelphia
museum features birds, mammals, and marine life,
including a paddlefish, the "1st Article of Museum,
1784."

☸ **Left: Copper admission token**
designed by Christian Gobrecht,
1821
Baltimore City Life Museums

Right: Copper admission token,
1825
Baltimore City Life Museums

Such tokens were used for admission to the Peale
museums in Philadelphia (left) and New York (right.)

educational affiliation, revolved around his efforts to publish a catalogue of the natural history specimens and later to write his lectures. According to the minutes of the library's board of directors, they decided in favor of "An application. . . made by Charles Wilson Peale for liberty to take home with him the works of Penna[n]t, Catesby, Latham, and other writers on natural history, in order to assist him in making out a Catalogue and description of the various articles in his Museum." In 1799 the directors granted Peale borrowing privileges once again for the preparation of his lectures, and this courtesy was renewed the following year. Peale expressed his gratitude in future years with gifts of his publications on health and moral life, "An Epistle to a Friend" (1803) and "An Essay to Promote Domestic Happiness" (1812). In reviewing Peale's alliances with Philadelphia's most prominent educational and scientific institutions, it seems evident that these connections helped support claims about the intellectual rigor of his endeavors. These affiliations also gained Peale access to the best educated and the recognized leaders in government, religion, commerce, and manufacturing, from whom Peale and the museum stood to benefit.[6]

In 1794, the year that Peale moved his museum into Philosophical Hall, he also began to keep a separate record of subscribers to tickets of annual admission. This is an extremely valuable source for documenting the individuals who comprised Peale's audience. Between 1794 and 1827, when Peale died, over 1,300 subscribers entered their names in this volume. Observations in this chapter are based upon a systematic study of the 401 people who signed their names in the first year that Peale maintained the book. Among those subscribers, more than one third shared Peale's interest in Philadelphia's three principal institutions of learning: the American Philosophical Society, the University of Pennsylvania, and the Library Company of Philadelphia. A total of 142 (35.4 percent) of Peale's subscribers were affiliated with at least one of these three institutions. Among those constituents, 94 (23.4 percent) were connected with just one of the three, 24 (6 percent) associated with two of the organizations, and another 24 (6 percent) with all three. Out of the 53 (13.2 percent) museum subscribers who were also members of the American Philosophical Society, 21 held offices in the society. Like Charles Willson Peale, five subscribers—William Bradford, Nicholas Collin, Zaccheus Collins, William Hembel, Jr., and David Rittenhouse—served as curators of the society. Among the affiliates of the university, the 66 (16.5 percent) men who comprise this group include non-degree earning matriculates; graduates who earned a B.A., B.M., A.M., M.D., LL.D., or D.D.; honorary degree recipients of the A.M., LL.D., or D.D.; and officers and professors of the university. The 95 (23.7 percent) subscribers identified with an interest in the Library Company of Philadelphia were all shareholders, which entitled them to borrowing privileges. The Library Company shareholders were socially broader than those associated with the other two institutions, and included a shopkeeper (William Hembel, Jr.), a printer (John Ormrod), an engraver (James Thackara), and a goldsmith (Rowland Parry).[7]

Peale moved beyond the singleness of purpose of academic affiliations by promoting the museum as capable of simultaneously amusing and instructing his audience. This concept blurred the lines between learning and leisure, and was a convention shared by promoters of both types of institutions. Burgiss Allison, a patron of Peale's museum and the operator of an academy for boys in Bordentown, New Jersey, shared Peale's belief in the consistency between these two activities. Allison advocated the introduction of dramatic texts to the classroom to more actively engage students' attention, as well as the bolder addition of instructive toys to the learning process. Cathy N. Davidson, in her study of novels and their readers in the early national period, shows that writers and publishers believed that a novel which amused and instructed would surely achieve commercial success. These examples demonstrate that the amuse/instruct unity was employed to promote educational and recreational activity, and that profit and learning were regarded as consistent enterprises.[8]

Peale's use of the phrases "rational entertainment" and "rational amusement" presents another view of the museum that combines learning with leisure. While similar in conception to the amuse/instruct construct, the phrase rational entertainment has a loaded place in the history of American leisure. In Quaker Philadelphia, as in other American cities, the theater was the most contested form of entertainment, and the term "rational amusement" was among the terms used to posit the merits of this cultural form. The Continental Congress in 1774 sought to reduce wasteful consumption by outlawing such activities as theatrical performances, cock

fighting, and elaborate funerals. The terms on which the theater was prohibited—"extravagance and dissipation"—set the moral tone that was maintained by the Pennsylvania legislature in its 1779 "Act for the Suppression of Vice and Immorality," which renewed the proscription of the theater in Pennsylvania. However, the General Assembly of Pennsylvania reversed itself in 1789, making the theater legal. Justifying this new openness to the theater, the law codified the terms of defensible leisure: citizens have a right, the law stated, to enjoy any "rational and innocent amusement, which at the same time, that it affords a necessary relaxation from the fatigues of business is calculated to inform the mind and improve the heart." Peale's use of the term rational entertainment, then, must be seen as not only promoting the museum as a boon to reason, but as a weapon against such social evils as vice, dissipation, and extravagance.[9]

Peale's effectiveness at defining the museum's mission in moral terms may be tested by his ability to coalesce the polar enemies in the theater debate. Quakers and clergymen directed the fight against the theater in 1793-1794, as they had in previous years. A substantial number of Quakers—John Ashbridge, the Bringhursts, Samuel Coates, Jasper Cope, the Cowperthwaites, Richard Hopkins, Thomas C. James, and the Marshalls, for example—were museum subscribers, but there is no evidence about their individual views on the theater issue. Among the ministers who petitioned against the theater but endorsed Peale were Thomas Fleeson, Ashbel Green, Henry Helmuth, William Marshall, Joseph Pilmore, John Blair Smith, William Smith, and William White.

Clergymen tolerant of the theater who subscribed to annual tickets were Nicholas Collin, Samuel Magaw, John Andrews, and John Ewing. Also among Peale's subscribers in 1794 was Henry Hill, the gentleman who orchestrated the pro-theater campaign on behalf of the stockholders of the New Theatre on Chestnut Street. Collin, the minister of the Gloria Dei, or Swedish, Church, was a particularly avid supporter of the museum, and later wrote a series of articles proclaiming the religious and moral worth of Peale's lectures on natural history.[10]

A contemporary Philadelphia guide book confirms that at least some portion of Peale's audience understood the museum as a model for the moral application of useful knowledge. According to this 1824 publication, Peale devoted the museum to

conveying instructions and amusement to his fellow citizens, and of advancing the interests of religion and morality, by the arrangement and display of the works of nature and art. The doors of the Museum have ever been closed against the profligate and the indecent, it has been preserved, with scrupulous fidelity, as a place where the virtuous and refined of society could meet to enjoy such pleasures as can be tasted by the virtuous and refined alone.

This brief passage is important because it identifies Peale with the goals that have been presented here as central to debates over education and entertainment—to amuse and instruct, to promote moral welfare, and to fight vice. This account also contributes a contemporary understanding of the composition of Peale's audience, proposing that his moral program was reserved for the "virtuous and refined of society," thereby excluding the lower classes.[11]

This understanding merits revision. Peale's moral stance implied a code of behavior that may be characterized as an important component of a middle-class ideology. The lessons to be learned from the museum were not simply about art and nature, but about social utility and contribution. Citizens were discouraged from immoral and therefore socially disruptive behavior. They were also discouraged from frivolous activity, which constituted socially useless pursuits. But the museum was open to people on the lower border of that class bloc, with the hope that they could be acculturated and thereby become less threatening. Rather than an exclusive model of participation, Peale encouraged all to attend, but to do so on the terms of amusement and instruction, rational amusement, and useful knowledge; that is, on the terms of middle class commitment to moral and productive living.[12]

Tax assessments for Peale's subscribers demonstrate that his patrons were indeed economically diverse, although slightly wealthier on average than contemporary Philadelphians. Of the 401 subscribers in 1794, tax assessments were located for 162. Ranging in wealth from no taxable assets to £9,703, Peale's patrons may be plotted on a fairly gradual scale of economic well-being. Peale's assessment of £401 placed him economically above two thirds of his subscribers. A comparison of the distribution of wealth among Peale's subscribers to all residents in Chestnut Ward in the 1790s demonstrates that museum goers belonged to a broad economic cross section of the population. Social historian Billy G. Smith has aggregated tax data for Chestnut Ward during selected years, which enables the evaluation of the subscribers' wealth relative to their fellow citizens. Whereas wealth was more highly concentrated among the highest decile of Chestnut Ward residents in 1795 than among Peale's 1794 subscribers, the distribution within Chestnut Ward for 1796 nearly mirrors the distribution for the 1794 subscribers. A principal difference between the two groups is that 80 percent of Peale's subscribers had at least some taxable wealth, while only 60 percent of Chestnut Ward residents were taxed for accumulated wealth in 1795 and 1796. However, the seventh and eighth deciles combined among Peale's patrons owned just 1 percent of the total wealth relative to the other subscribers. Tax assessments divided taxable wealth into eight categories. Ownership of cows was distributed among the top six deciles of Peale's subscribers. Members of the top eight deciles owned one or more horses, with all sixteen members of the top decile taxed in this category and just one subscriber taxed for a horse in the eighth decile. Riding equipment was distributed among the top seven deciles, and varied from William Bingham's assessment for a coach (£90), a chariot (£75), a coachee (£50), and a sulky (£10) to Josiah Hewes's more modest assessment for a chair (£15). Assessments for plate or precious metal were similarly concentrated in the top decile and decreased steadily into the eighth decile. Assessments for indentured servants were more evenly distributed among the top eight deciles. In contrast to the 24.3 percent concentration of assessments on indentured ser-

vants among the top decile, 51.9 percent of slave ownership was within the top decile of Peale's subscribers. Personal tax, levied according to one's occupation, was the most evenly distributed category among Peale's subscribers. Real estate, which comprised 78.1 percent of all wealth among Peale's subscribers, was the most highly concentrated asset among the top decile and was owned only by members of the top four deciles. In comparison to Peale's subscribers, just the top two deciles among those taxed in Chestnut Ward owned real estate. This distinction indicates that a higher proportion of Peale's subscribers owned real estate—the single most important economic distinction in early national Philadelphia—than typical residents in the city. Although tax assessments for the bottom 20 percent of Peale's subscribers reveal no accumulated wealth, the lowest two deciles included men of respectable occupation: attorney William H. Tod, doctor Stephen Le Breton, minister James Abercrombie, and United States Congressman Samuel Griffin.[13]

Whereas tax assessments suggest that Peale's patrons were only slightly wealthier than average Philadelphians, a comparison of the identified occupations of Peale's subscribers indicates that they were of significantly higher status than average contemporary Philadelphians. Stuart Blumin's recent history of the American middle class divides the early national occupational structure into four levels—high non-manual, low non-manual, high manual, and low manual—with the middle two categories forming the "middling sort." Despite Peale's frequent identification in the literature with Philadelphia's artisan culture, both skilled craftsmen and unskilled laborers were vastly underrepresented among the subscribers. In contrast to the 62.3 percent of Peale's patrons who worked in high non-manual occupations, Blumin found that just 22.1 percent of Philadelphians were similarly employed. The 25.6 percent representation of Peale's audience in low non-manual positions compares closely to the 27.4 percent proposed by Blumin for their contemporaries. The most startling contrast, however, is between 40.5 percent high manual and 10 percent low manual workers estimated for all Philadelphia and the 12.1 percent high manual and 0 percent low manual among Peale's subscribers. In contemporary terms, the upper sort were vastly overrepresented among Peale's subscribers, while the middling sort were underrepresented and the lower sort were absent.[14]

Peale's fee structures contributed to this apparent exclusion of the socially lower and contradicted his expressed hopes of moral uplift through the museum's lessons. When Peale expanded his museum into the Pennsylvania State House in 1802, he maintained quarters in Philosophical Hall as well. Later in the year, he introduced the mastodon, or "mammoth," exhibit at Philosophical Hall. The separate locations enabled him to charge 25 cents to the museum in the State House, and another 50 cents to the mastodon and other exhibits in Philosophical Hall. Contemporary visitors' accounts confirm that some viewers were excluded by the additional charge. Catherine Fritsch wrote, "All this time I was looking forward to seeing the mammoth, and now I proposed that we inquire for it. Then a gentleman who had just come from Philosophical Hall, where the great skeleton was kept, told us that he had seen it and had to pay 1/2 dollar for the privilege. All the party, but myself, declared that the price was entirely too high—a quarter they would give willingly, but not a cent more!" Billy G. Smith's careful analysis of the income and expenditures of working people—laborers, mariners, cordwainers, and tailors—indicates that Peale's fees were likely prohibitive to some members of the "lower sort." Cathy Davidson's work on book distribution suggests that even inexpensive novels, costing 75 cents to $1.50, were beyond the means of the working class. Peale's fees for annual tickets required a larger cash outlay and constituted an even more exclusive form of patronage. These tickets first sold for $1, then $2, $5, $6, and by 1819 $10. To those who paid for annual tickets, Peale reserved a special title—"the Friends of Science"—and promised that their names would be handed down to posterity through the subscription book.[15]

Admission fees and the arrangement of Philadelphia theater interiors similarly demarcated tripartite social distinctions of wealth among its audience. The most expensive and fashionable seats were at stage level, the middle-priced seats were below stage level, and the cheapest seats were above stage level. This structure separated the classes into distinct spaces, but also inverted the hierarchy among the lower and the middling people: socially higher were seated spatially lower. Occasionally this contradiction erupted into riotous conflict. "A Frequenter of the Theatre" complained in the newspaper that the "boys of the Gallery," the occupants of the cheapest seats, demanded deferential behavior from the middling sort in the pit. If the middle class did not comply with demands to remove their hats and bow to their social inferiors, they were pummeled with abusive language, beer, spit, fruit, sticks, and stones.[16]

Although Peale's open admission policy aimed at controlling just such rowdiness among the lower sort, viewers' behavior sometimes subverted, albeit unintentionally, his goals of moral uplift. Resistance to Peale's program may be discerned in acts of graffiti and defacement of displays. Peale complained of his audience's offensive behavior to his son Rembrandt:

> You know how much we have [been] pestered by persons going down from the Museum in ringing the bells, it is completely cured by my writing in large letters, facing them in their de[s]cent. "None but the Rude and uncultivated ring the Bells going down." I wish I could also prevent visitors from puting their fingers on the Glasses and frames in the different parts of the Museum, they dirty the glass and destroy the brilliency of the gilding.

> The standing on our covered benches is another dirty custom, could I be often in the museum I should prevent it as I sometimes do taking out my Handkerchief and wiping & brushing after them, without uttering a sylable. I have just thought that I might put into conspicuous places, frames on containing requests that Visitors may not scratch their names on the Chama's [shells], Pensil or nor mutilate the Casts, sully the Glass or frames with their fingers, nor stand on the covered benches, as Stepes are provided to raise them to the sight of high Objects, that it must be obvious to every thinking being that these rules are necessary to preserve the articles of a Museum formed for the instruction and amusement of the present as well as future generations.

If the museum taught morals through the arrangement of the exhibits and by a code of expected behavior, these acts disrupted the order upon which those lessons were predicated.[17] ❀ ❀ ❀

Notes

Frequently Cited Sources

Lillian B. Miller, ed., *The Collected Papers of Charles Willson Peale and His Family, 1735-1885* (Millwood, New York: Kraus Microform, 1980, microfiche), hereinafter Miller, *Collected Papers.*

Lillian B. Miller and others, eds., *The Selected Papers of Charles Willson Peale and His Family,* 3 vols. (New Haven: Yale University Press for the National Portrait Gallery, Smithsonian Institution, 1983, 1988, and 1991), hereinafter Miller, *Selected Papers.*

Joel J. Orosz, *Curators and Culture: The Museum Movement in America,1740-1870* (Tuscaloosa: The University of Alabama Press, 1990), hereinafter Orosz, *Curators and Culture.*

Peale-Sellers Papers, in the American Philosophical Society Library, Philadelphia, hereinafter Peale-Sellers Papers.

Charles Coleman Sellers, *Charles Willson Peale* (New York: Charles Scribner's Sons, 1969), hereinafter Sellers, *Charles Wilson Peale.*

Charles Coleman Sellers, *Mr. Peale's Museum: Charles Willson Peale and the First Popular Museum of Natural Science and Art* (New York: W.W. Norton & Co., Inc., 1980), hereinafter Sellers, *Mr. Peale's Museum.*

Introduction
Gary Kulik

1. Sellers, *Charles Willson Peale* and his *Mr. Peale's Museum;* Edgar P. Richardson, Brooke Hindle, and Lillian B. Miller, *Charles Willson Peale and His World* (N. Y.: Charles N. Abrams, 1983); Roger B. Stein, "Charles Willson Peale's Expressive Design: The Artist in His Museum," *Prospects,* 6 (1981), 129-85; Gary Kulik, "Designing the Past: History Museum Exhibitions From Peale to the Present," in Warren Leon and Roy Rosenzweig, eds., *History Museums in the United States: A Critical Assessment* (Urbana, Ill.: University of Illinois Press, 1989), 2-37. See also the portraits of Peale in Edward P. Alexander, *Museum Masters: Their Museums and Their Influence* (Nashville: American Association for State and Local History, 1983); Joseph J. Ellis, *After the Revolution: Profiles of Early American Culture* (N. Y.: W.W. Norton & Co., Inc., 1979), and Orosz, *Curators and Culture.*

The latest exhibition on the Peales is the Peale Museum's "Mermaids, Mummies, and Mastodons: The Evolution of the American Museum," reviewed in this volume by Edward P. Alexander and by Gary Kulik in the *Journal of American History,* 78 (June 1991), 255-9. The most recent publication of the Peale Papers Project of the National Portrait Gallery is *The Selected Papers of Charles Willson Peale and His Family,* Vol. 3, *The Belfield Farm Years, 1810-1820,* eds., Lillian B. Miller, Sidney Hart, David C. Ward, and Rose S. Emerick (New Haven: Yale University Press, 1991).

2. Michael S. Shapiro, ed., *The Museum: A Reference Guide* (Westport, Conn.: Greenwood Press, 1989).

3. Quoted in Ruth Helm, "Peale's Museum: Politics, Idealism, and Public Patronage in the Early Republic," in this volume.

4. Gary Kulik, "History Museums and the Cultural Politics of the 1980s," *History News*, 45 (May/June 1990): 22-24.

5. Casey Nelson Blake, "Whose Right to Public Art and Public Space? The Controversy Over Richard Serra's 'Tilted Arc,' 1981-89," paper given at the American Studies Association meeting, 1991.

6. Lawrence W. Levine, *Highbrow/Lowbrow: The Emergence of Cultural Hierarchy in the United States* (Cambridge, Mass.: Harvard University Press, 1988).

7. See A. Hunter Dupree, *Science in the Federal Government: A History of Policies and Activities* (Cambridge, Mass.: Harvard University Press, 1957); Wilcomb E. Washburn, "Joseph Henry's Conception of the Purpose of the Smithsonian Institution," in Whitfield Bell, et. al., *A Cabinet of Curiosities: Five Episodes in the Evolution of American Museums* (Charlottesville: University Press of Virginia, 1967), 106-66; Nathan Reingold, "The New York State Roots of Joseph Henry's National Career," *New York History*, 59 (April, 1973), 132-44.

8. The mission statement is from the Canadian Museum of Civilization in Hull, Ottawa.

Entrepreneurs and Intellectuals: Natural History in Early American Museums
Sally Gregory Kohlstedt

1. I wish to acknowledge support from a Woodrow Wilson Center fellowship which helped me acquire information for this essay at the Library of Congress and at various facilities in Baltimore.

2. John C. Greene, *American Science in the Age of Jefferson* (Ames: Iowa State University, 1984).

3. Sally Gregory Kohlstedt, "Parlors, Primers, and Public Schooling: Education for Science in Early America," *Isis,* 81 (Fall, 1990): 424-45.

4. The quotation is from Charles Willson Peale's *A Scientific and Descriptive Catalogue of Peale's Museum* (Philadelphia: Samuel H. Smith [1796]). For a discussion of attitudes toward technology, see John Kasson, *Civilizing the Machine: Technology and Republican Values in America, 1776-1900* (New York: Grossman, 1976). See Miller, *Collected Papers* and Sellers, *Mr. Peale's Museum.* For an important predecessor, see Joel J. Orosz, "Pierre Eugene Du Simitiere: Museum Pioneer in America," *Museum Studies Journal* 1 (Spring, 1985): 8-18. Orosz, *Curators and Culture.*

5. Toby A. Appel, "Science, Popular Culture, and Profit: Peale's Philadelphia Museum," *Society for the Bibliography of Natural History,* 9 (April, 1980): 619-34.

6. Charlotte M.. Porter, *The Eagle's Nest: Natural History and American Ideas, 1812-1842* (Tuscaloosa: University of Alabama Press, 1986).

7. Quoted in J. Thomas Scharf and Thompson Westcott, *History of Philadelphia, 1609-1884,* 2 (Philadelphia: I. H. Everts and Co., 1884): 950.

8. *Monthly Miscellany and Boston Review,* 1 (1804): 240.

9. Antonello Gerbi, *The Dispute of the New World: The History of a Polemic, 1750-1900,* trans. Jeremy Moyle (Pittsburgh: University of Pittsburgh Press, 1973).

10. For an account of such efforts see essays in Alexandra Oleson and Sanborn Brown, *The Pursuit of Knowledge in the Early American Republic: American Scientific and Learned Societies from Colonial Times to the Civil War* (Baltimore: The Johns Hopkins University Press, 1976). See also Simon Baatz, *Knowledge, Culture, and Science in the Metropolis: The New York Academy*

of Sciences, 1817-1970, published in *Annals of the New York Academy of Sciences,* 584 (1990).

11. Wilbur H. Hunter, Jr., "The Tribulations of a Museum Director in the 1820s," *Maryland Historical Magazine,* 49 (1954): 219.

12. Bachman to [?], draft letter, 8 May 1843, Bachman MSS, Charleston Museum.

13. Dr. R.. M. Strong, "In Retrospect" (copy in Milwaukee Public Library Archives); C. H. Doerflinger, *The Genesis and Early History of the Wisconsin Natural History Society at Milwaukee* (n.p., [1907]).

14. Edward Lurie, *Louis Agassiz: A Life in Science* (Chicago: University of Chicago Press, 1966).

15. Sally Gregory Kohlstedt, "From Learned Society to Public Museum: The Boston Society of Natural History," in Alexandra Oleson and John Voss, eds., *The Organization of Knowledge in Modern America, 1860-1920* (Baltimore: Johns Hopkins University Press, 1979), 386-476. John Michael Kennedy, *Philanthropy and Science in New York City: The American Museum of Natural History, 1868-1968* (Ph.D. diss., Yale University, 1968).

16. For more information on the predilections of science during this period see Robert V. Bruce, *The Launching of Modern American Science, 1846-1876* (New York: Alfred A. Knopf, 1987).

17. Sally Gregory Kohlstedt, "Museums on Campus: A Tradition of Inquiry and Teaching," in Ron Rainger, Keith Benson, and Jane Maienschein, eds., *The American Development of Biology* (Philadelphia: University of Pennsylvania Press, 1988), 15-47.

18. *The Origins of Natural Science in the United States: The Essays of George Brown Goode,* ed. Sally Gregory Kohlstedt (Washington, D.C.: Smithsonian Institution Press, 1991); and also Edward P. Alexander, "George Brown Goode and the Smithsonian Museums: A National Museum of Cultural History," in *Museum Masters: Their Museums and Influence* (Nash-

ville: American Association for State and Local History, 1983), 277-309.

In Pursuit of a Profit
John W. Durel

1. Charles Willson Peale to Rubens Peale, 6 November 1818, Peale-Sellers Papers.

2. The timeline published here was produced originally for the exhibit "Mermaids, Mummies, and Mastodons." The research and writing was done by Richard Flint, curator of the exhibit, with the assistance of a host of museum staff and volunteer researchers. The timeline integrates museum records with other sources, including local newspapers, travellers' accounts, and correspondence, to give a longitudinal picture of the museum's operation.

3. Rubens Peale to Benjamin Franklin Peale, 9 July 1822, Peale-Sellers Papers.

4. Rubens Peale to Benjamin Franklin Peale, 26 August 1822, and Rubens Peale to Benjamin Franklin Peale, 12 December 1822, Peale-Sellers Papers.

5. For information on Padihershef see R. Jackson Wilson, "Thebes to Springfield: The Travels of an Egyptian Mummy," *Padihershef, the Egyptian Mummy* (Springfield, Mass.: George Walter Vincent Smith Art Museum, 1984). The financial arrangements are in Rubens Peale's Museum Account Book, Maryland Historical Society.

6. Charles Willson Peale to Rembrandt Peale, June 1823, Peale-Sellers Papers.

7. Rubens Peale to Rembrandt Peale, 18 August 1824; Rubens Peale to Eliza Peale, 5 September 1824, Peale-Sellers Papers. See also Wilbur H. Hunter, Jr., "The Tribulations of a Museum Director in the 1820s," *Maryland Historical Magazine,* 49 (1954): 214-22.

8. The title and description of the museum in the Bill of Sale, October 31, 1828. Peale-Sellers Papers.

Politics, Idealism, and Public Patronage in the Early Republic
Ruth Helm

1. Charles Willson Peale, hereinafter CWP, Autobiography, Peale-Sellers Papers. Also included in Miller, *Collected Papers,* which contains many of the Peale-Sellers Papers.

2. Benjamin Rush to ?, 25 May 1786, quoted in Charles Coleman Sellers, *Charles Willson Peale,* 212.

3. *Pennsylvania Packet,* 7 July 1786; CWP to George Washington, 27 June 1790, Peale-Sellers Papers; CWP to [Tobias] Lear, 23 March 1792, Peale-Sellers Papers.

4. Republicanism, the prevailing ideology of the Revolutionary period, assumed in part, the full participation in civic life of enlightened, independent citizens; for a complete discussion of republican ideology, see Gordon S. Wood, *The Creation of the American Republic, 1776-1787* (New York: W.W. Norton, 1969), chap. 2 and *passim.*

5. *Gentleman's Magazine* 18 (1748): 302; also quoted in Edward Miller, *That Noble Cabinet: A History of the British Museum* (Athens, OH: Ohio University Press, 1974), 40.

6. CWP, "To the Citizens of the United States of America," 1 February 1790, George Washington Papers, Library of Congress.

7. CWP to John Hawkins, 3 March 1807, Peale-Sellers Papers.

8. CWP to James Madison, 30 April 1809, Peale-Sellers Papers.

9. CWP to George Washington, 27 June 1790, see n.3.

10. CWP to James Madison, 24 May 1801, Peale-Sellers Papers.

11. CWP to Thomas Jefferson, 12 January, 1802, Peale-Sellers Papers.

12. Sellers, *Charles Willson Peale,* 240.

13. Thomas Jefferson to CWP, 16 January 1802, Hanley Collection, Humanities Research Center, University of Texas at Austin.

14. Charleston *Columbian Herald,* 23 September 1785; "Sober Citizen," *To the Inhabitants of the City and County of New York,* 16 April 1776; ? Coleman, *Revolution in Georgia,* 85; all quoted in Wood, *Creation of the American Republic,* 477; also see Jackson Turner Main, "Government by the People: The American Revolution and the Democratization of the Legislatures," *William and Mary Quarterly* 3rd series, 23 (July 1966): 391-407.

15. CWP to Rembrandt Peale, 8 January 1819, Peale-Sellers Papers.

16. CWP to Thomas Jefferson, 1 January 1819, Peale-Sellers Papers.

17. Thomas Jefferson to CWP, 15 February 1824, Tracy W. McGregor Collection, University of Virginia Library, Charlottesville.

18. Thomas Jefferson to CWP, 16 January 1802, Hanly Collection, U. of Texas.

19. CWP to Board of Visitors of the Philadelphia Museum, [June 1792], Peale-Sellers Papers.

20. CWP to William Bingham, 1 April [17]92; CWP to Miers Fisher, [April 1792], Peale-Sellers Papers.

21. CWP to Robert Lesley, 26 July 1795, Peale-Sellers Papers.

22. CWP to Timothy Matlack, 9 March 1800; CWP to Mr. Finley [William Findley], 18 February, 1800, Peale-Sellers Papers.

23. CWP to Mr. Finley, see n.22.

24. CWP to Thomas McKean, 3 March 1800, Peale-Sellers Papers.

25. Sellers, *Mr. Peale's Museum,* 112.

26. CWP to Thomas McKean, see n.24; almost immediately, Peale solicited the assistance of the national government; see n.10 and 11.

27. CWP to Thomas Jefferson, 21 January 1802, Library of Congress; also 20 January 1802, Peale-Sellers Papers.

28. Sellers, *Mr. Peale's Museum,* 152; also see CWP to Andrew Ellicott, 28 February 1802, Peale-Sellers Papers.

29. CWP to Andrew Ellicott, see n.28.

30. CWP to the Common Council of the City of Philadelphia, 11 March 1802, Peale-Sellers Papers.

31. CWP to Elisha Gordon, 11 March 1802, Peale-Sellers Papers.

32. Sellers, *Mr. Peale's Museum,* 195. The remainder of the building would be converted into fireproof offices for city and county records.

33. CWP to Rubens Peale, 25 February 1810, Peale-Sellers Papers. The Legislature certainly anticipated the permanent establishment of Harrisburg as the capital of Pennsylvania in 1812, leaving the old State House at Philadelphia with no official function.

34. CWP to Simon Snyder, 5 January 1812, Peale-Sellers Papers.

35. CWP to Charles Biddle, 3 March 1812, Peale-Sellers Papers; see also, for instance, CWP to George Washington, n.3.

36. CWP to Rembrandt Peale, 10 July 1816, Peale-Sellers Papers.

37. CWP to Angelica Peale Robinson, 8 July 1816, CWP to Rembrandt Peale, 10 July 1816, Peale-Sellers Papers.

38. Sellers, *Mr. Peale's Museum,* 232.

39. CWP to the Honorable the Select and Common Councils of the City of Philadelphia, 10 April 1817, Peale-Sellers Papers.

40. CWP to Rembrandt Peale, 21 May 1817; CWP to Thomas Jefferson, 20 May 1817, Peale-Sellers Papers.

41. CWP to Rembrandt Peale, see n.40.

42. CWP to Thomas Jefferson, see n.40.

43. Report of the Committee of the Select and Common Councils, 13 January 1818, Historical Society of Pennsylvania, Philadelphia, in Miller, *Collected Papers.*

44. CWP to Thomas Jefferson, 15 January 1818, Peale-Sellers Papers.

45. CWP to [The Select and Common Councils of Philadelphia], 8 November 1820, Autograph File, Houghton Library, Harvard University, Cambridge, Mass. in Miller, *Collected Papers.*

46. CWP to Rachel Morris, 13 April 1824, Peale-Sellers Papers; Peale had incorporated the Philadelphia Museum in 1821, and appointed a supervisory board of trustees.

47. Ruth Helm, "'For Credit, Honor, and Profit': Three Generations of the Peale Family in America" (Ph.D. diss., University of Colorado, 1991), 141-46; also see Sidney Hart and David C. Ward, "The Waning of an Enlightenment Ideal: Charles Willson Peale's Philadelphia Museum, 1790-1820," in *Journal of the Early Republic* 8 (Winter 1988).

48. CWP to Simon Snyder, 5 January 1812, Peale-Sellers Papers.

49. CWP to Rembrandt Peale, 10 July 1816, Peale-Sellers Papers.

50. CWP to Rembrandt Peale, 27 July 1812, Peale-Sellers Papers.

51. CWP to James Madison, 21 May 1801; CWP to Rubens Peale and Sophonisba Peale Sellers, 19 January 1805; CWP to James Monroe, 21 February 1824, Peale-Sellers Papers.

52. Rembrandt Peale studied painting in Paris in 1808 and again in 1809-10. He was thus familiar with the works of Jacques-Louis David and Francois Gerard whose composition he was charged with copying; see Sellers, *Charles Willson Peale,* 360-61.

53. With his brother Raphaelle, Rembrandt had attempted to open a small gallery in Baltimore in 1796. Intended to generate orders for portraits as well as display paintings, artifacts, and preserved specimens, this museum found little favor in the city and closed in 1798.

54. CWP to Rembrandt Peale, 27 July 1812, Peale-Sellers Papers.

55. CWP to [Nathaniel] Ramsay, 13 March 1813, Peale-Sellers Papers.

56. *Ibid.;* CWP to Rembrandt Peale, 6 September 1814, Peale-Sellers Papers; MF; Rembrandt would later claim his aversion to "the *GOD* of this country— *Money,*" and denounce Baltimore for "the sordid calculations of shortsighted commercial avarice" that undermined the purposes of the museum; see Rembrandt Peale to Charles Mayer, 12 October 1830, Peale Family Collection, MS 1935, Maryland Historical Society, Baltimore.

57. CWP to Dr. Hosack, 29 June 1805, Peale-Sellers Papers.

58. Ibid.; *American and Commercial Advertiser,* Baltimore, 15 August 1814; quoted in Sellers, *Charles Willson Peale* 362, 475, n.28; see also Sellers, *Mr. Peale's Museum,* 222.

59. Rembrandt Peale to Thomas Jefferson, 13 July 1813, Coolidge Collection, Massachusetts Historical Society, Boston.

60. *American and Commercial Advertises,* see n. 59; Sellers, *Mr. Peale's Museum,* 222; John H. B. Latrobe, quoted in Raphael Semmes, "Baltimore During the Time of the Old Peale Museum," *Maryland Historical Magazine* 27 (1932):115.

61. Helm, "'For Credit, Honor, and Profit," chap. 5, passim.

62. CWP to [Nathaniel] Ramsay, see n.56.

63. CWP to John Beale Bordley, 5 December 1786, Peale-Sellers Papers.

64. CWP to [Nathaniel] Ramsay, see n.56.

65. CWP to John C. Calhoun, 30 August 1822, Peale-Sellers Papers.

Social Class and Participation in Peale's Philadelphia Museum
David R. Brigham

A version of this paper was presented at the annual meeting of the American Studies Association, 2 November 1991. I would like to thank Gary Kulik, Elizabeth Johns, and Amy Henderson for their comments on earlier drafts of this essay.

I am grateful to The Peale Family Papers, National Portrait Gallery, for the use of their research files. All references to newspapers other than the *General Advertiser* and the *Aurora General Advertiser* are from photocopies in their files.

This research has been supported generously by predoctoral fellowships from the Philadelphia Center for Early American Studies and the Smithsonian Institution.

1. Charles Willson Peale, memorial to the state legislature of Pennsylvania , in *Poulson's American Daily Advertiser,* l8 December 1810; Orosz, *Curators and Culture,* 49-50; and Sidney Hart and David C. Ward, "The Waning of an Enlightenment Ideal: Charles Willson Peale's Philadelphia Museum 1790-1820," in Lillian B. Miller and David C. Ward, eds., *New Perspectives on Charles Willson Peale: A 250th Anniversary Celebration* (Pittsburgh: University of Pittsburgh Press for the Smithsonian Institution, 1991), 221-22.

2. "On the FOLLY of ENGAGING in TRIFLING STUDIES," *General Advertiser,* 14 August, 1794, from the *Columbian Magazine;* "The Unhappiness consequent on the Neglect of early improving the Mind [addressed to youth]," *General Advertiser,* 10 December 1790.

Peale's return to the museum and the commission of *The Artist in His Museum* in 1822 is treated in Sellers *Mr. Peale's Museum,* 240, 246. Peale's interest in false teeth is discussed in Sidney Hart, " 'To encrease the comforts of life': Charles Willson Peale and the Mechanical Arts," *Pennsylvania Magazine of History and Biography,* vol. 110, no. 3 (July 1986): 332-34.

3. Peale's opening announcement, *The Pennsylvania Packet,* 7 July 1786, is reproduced in Miller, *Selected Papers* vol. 1, p. 448.

Peale's election to the American Philosophical Society, *Pennsylvania Packet,* 25 July 1786.

The years of Peale's tenure as curator are established by the membership card file in the library of the American Philosophical Society. Co-curators are named in annual publications of the officers of the society, including *The Pennsylvania Packet,* 18 January, 1788; *General Advertiser and Political, Commercial and Literary Journal,* 12 January, 1791; *General Advertiser,* 9 January 1792, 8 January 1793, 13 January 1794; *Aurora General Advertiser,* 9 January 1795, 21 January 1796, 13 January 1797, 8 January 1799, 6 January 1800, 6 January 1801, 5 January 1802, 10 January 1803, 13 January 1804, 7 January 1805, 7 January 1806, 3 January 1807, 2 January 1808, and 7 January 1809; *Philadelphia Gazette,* 19 January 1798.

The curator's role as librarian is described in Murphy D. Smith, *Oak from an Acorn: A History of the American Philosophical Society Library, 1770-1803* (Wilmington: Scholarly Resources, 1976),19-20. I would like to thank Roy E. Goodman for this citation.

On Du Simitiere, Paul Ginsburg Sifton, "Pierre Eugene Du Simitiere (1737-1784): Collector in Revolutionary America," Ph.D. diss., University of Pennsylvania, Philadelphia, 1960; and Orosz, *Curators and Culture,* 30-44.

Peale announced his move into Philosophical Hall in the *General Advertiser,* 19 September 1794, reproduced in Miller, *Selected Papers* vol. 2, part 1, p. 98. Charles Coleman Sellers suggests that the museum was situated there by 15 July 1794, in his *Charles Willson Peale,* 265.

4. University as tenant, Martin Meyerson and Dilys Pegler Winegrad, *Gladly Learn and Gladly Teach: Franklin and His Heirs at the University of Pennsylvania, 1740-1976* (Philadelphia: University of Pennsylvania Press, 1978), 240; lectures in the hall of the university, *Aurora General Advertiser,* 14 November 1799 and 8 November 1800; Charles Caldwell's lectures, *Poulson's American Daily Advertiser,* 15 April 1818.

5. Acknowledgements of Patterson's gift include Charles Willson Peale, "Introduction to a Course of Lectures on Natural History Delivered in the University of Pennsylvania, November 16, 1799," in Miller, *Selected Papers,* vol. 2, pt. 1, p. 269, and Charles Willson Peale, "Address Delivered by Charles W. Peale, to the Corporation and Citizens of Philadelphia, on the 18th Day of July, 1816, in Academy Hall, Fourth Street" (Philadelphia: Printed for the Author, 1816), 7.

The inscription on *The Artist in His Museum* was recorded from my examination of a color transparency. As it hangs in the Pennsylvania Academy of the

Fine Arts, the inscription is partially covered by the frame.

For discussions of the politics of the 1792 committee, Sellers, *Mr. Peale's Museum*, 56-61; Miller, *Selected Papers*, vol. 2, pt. 1, pp. 19, 24; and Orosz, *Curators and Culture*, 53-54.

6. Charles Willson Peale to the Directors of the Library Company of Philadelphia, 5 October 1795, in Miller, *Selected Papers*, vol. 2, pt. 1, pp. 126-27. Acknowledgement of the request and permission to use one book at a time, Minutes of the Directors of the Library Company of Philadelphia (hereinafter Minutes LCP) 5 November 1795, MS, Library Company of Philadelphia; extension of borrowing privileges, Minutes LCP, 6 April 1797.

French version of the first and only section of the catalogue to be published, A.M.F.J. Palisot de Beauvois, "Catalogue Raisonné du Museum de Mr. C.W. Peale (Philadelphia: Printed by Peter Parent, 1796); English version, Charles Willson Peale and A.M.F.J. Palisot de Beauvois, "Scientific and Descriptive Catalogue of Peale's Museum," (Philadelphia: Printed by Samuel H. Smith, 1796).

Peale's request to use the library for his lectures, Minutes LCP, 12 December 1799; for the following season, Minutes LCP, 7 August 1800.

Charles Willson Peale, "An Epistle to a Friend, on the Means of Preserving Health, Promoting Happiness, and Prolonging the Life of Man to its Natural Period," (Philadelphia: From the press of the late R. Aitken by Jane Aitken, 1803), in Miller, *Selected Papers*, vol. 2, pt. 1, pp. 491-513; gift of this pamphlet to the Library Company, Minutes LCP, 3 March 1803.

Charles Willson Peale, "An Essay to Promote Domestic Happiness," (Philadelphia: Sold by Kimber & Conrad, J. Johnson, J.P. Park, T. Dobson, and at the Philadelphia Museum, 1812); for the gift to the Library Company, Minutes LCP, 6 August 1812.

I would like to thank Gordon Marshall and John C. Van Horne of the Library Company of Philadelphia for sharing their gleanings with me from the minutes of the directors.

7. *Subscriptions for Tickets in Peale's Museum*, 1794-1833, MS vol., Historical Society of Pennsylvania. Prior record of subscribers includes a list compiled at the end of Peale's Diary, 7 August-13 December 1790, in Miller, *Collected Papers*, IIB/11B2.

American Philosophical Society membership: American Philosophical Society, *Year Book 1985* (Philadelphia: American Philosophical Society, 1986) and the membership card file in the library of the society.

University of Pennsylvania affiliation: University of Pennsylvania, Society of the Alumni, *Biographical Catalogue of the Matriculates of the College* (Philadelphia: Printed for the Society, 1894); University of Pennsylvania, Society of the Alumni of the Medical Department, *Catalogue of the Alumni of the Medical Department of the University of Pennsylvania 1765-1877* (Philadelphia: Printed by Collins, 1877); and University of Pennsylvania, *Alumni Master File*, microfilm, University of Pennsylvania Archives.

Library Company of Philadelphia shareholding: Zachariah Poulson, Jr., compiler, *A Chronological Register of the Names of the Members of the Library Company of Philadelphia . . .*, begun ca. 1800, ms. vol., Library Company of Philadelphia.

8. Peale's aspiration toward "instruction as well as amusement," *General Advertiser*, 11 March 1793. Orosz treats Peale's interest in this concept in *Curators and Culture*, 80-85.

Burgiss Allison to Benjamin Rush, 2 July 1792, in *General Advertiser*, 10 October 1792, from the *Universal Asylum*.

Cathy N. Davidson, *Revolution and the Word: The Rise of the Novel in America* (New York and Oxford: Oxford University Press, 1986), 66, 70.

9. Peale and "rational entertainment," *General Advertiser*, 22 August 1794, and *Aurora General Advertiser*, 26 December 1796.

United States, Continental Congress, *Journal of the Proceedings of the Congress, Held at Philadelphia, Septem-*

ber 5, 1774 (Philadelphia: William and Thomas Bradford, 1774), 72.

Pennsylvania, General Assembly, "An ACT for the suppression of vice and immorality," *Laws Enacted in the Second Sitting of the Third General Assembly, of the Commonwealth of Pennsylvania, Which Commenced at Philadelphia, on Monday the First Day of February, A.D. One Thousand Seven Hundred and Seventy Nine, and Continued Till Monday the Fifth Day of April of the Same Year* (Philadelphia: Printed by John Dunlap, 1779), 190-93. Pennsylvania, General Assembly, "An ACT to repeal so much of an Act of General Assembly of this Commonwealth, as prohibits Dramatic Entertainments within the City of Philadelphia and the Neighborhood thereof," *Laws of the Thirteenth General Assembly of the Commonwealth of Pennsylvania, Enacted in the Second Sitting . . . .* (Philadelphia: Printed by Thomas Bradford, [1789]), 14-15.

10. Quaker membership is ascribed through William Wade Hinshaw and Thomas Worth Marshall, compilers, *Encyclopedia of American Quaker Genealogy,* 7 vols. (Ann Arbor, Michigan: Edwards Brothers, Inc., 1938) vol. 2.

Anti-theater ministers: *General Advertiser,* 27 December 1793; pro-theater ministers: *General Advertiser,* 17 December 1793 and 30 December 1793.

Henry Hill, *General Advertiser,* 1 January 1794.

Nicholas Collin, see Miller, *Selected Papers,* vol. 2, pt. 1, p. 49; and *Poulson's American Daily Advertiser,* 17, 18, 19, 20, 23, and 24 December, 1800.

11. *Philadelphia in 1824 . . . .* (Philadelphia: H.C. Carey and I. Lea, August, 1824), 101-102. I would like to thank Tony Lewis for sharing this account with me.

12. Joel J. Orosz also sees the museum intended as a tool for moral uplift in *Curators and Culture,* 51.

13. Philadelphia County Tax Assessment Ledgers, 1794-1797, MS vols., Philadelphia City Archives. Assessments were gathered for subscribers in Chestnut, Dock, High Street, Lower Delaware, Middle, New Market, North, North Mulberry, South, South Mulberry, Upper Delaware, and Walnut wards. Further investigation in the ledgers of the 13 additional townships and districts that comprised Philadelphia county would reveal more subscribers' assessments. The vast majority of the assessments were found in the 1794 ledgers.

Billy G. Smith's discussion of the distribution of wealth in Chestnut Ward is in *The "Lower Sort": Philadelphia's Laboring People, 1750-1800* (Ithaca and London: Cornell University Press, 1990), 224-29.

14. The occupations of Peale's subscribers were determined through the following sources: Clement Biddle, *The Philadelphia Directory* (Philadelphia: Printed by James & Johnson, 1791); James Hardie, *The Philadelphia Directory and Register* (Philadelphia: Printed by T. Dobson, 1793); James Hardie, *The Philadelphia Directory and Register,* 2nd ed. (Philadelphia: Printed by Jacob Johnson & Co., 1794); Edmund Hogan, *The Prospect of Philadelphia* (Philadelphia: Printed by Francis and Robert Bailey, 1795); Thomas Stephens, *Stephens's Philadelphia Directory for 1796* (Philadelphia: Printed for Thomas Stephens by W. Woodward, 1796); Cornelius W. Stafford, *The Philadelphia Directory for 1797* (Philadelphia: Printed by William W. Woodward, 1797); Cornelius W. Stafford, *The Philadelphia Directory for 1798* (Philadelphia: Printed by William W. Woodward, 1798); Cornelius W. Stafford, *The Philadelphia Directory for 1800* (Philadelphia: Printed by William W. Woodward, 1800); James Robinson, *The Philadelphia Directory for 1804* (Philadelphia: Printed by John H. Oswald, 1804); Philadelphia County Tax Assessment Ledgers, 1794-1797, MS vols., Philadelphia City Archives; Enumeration of Taxable Citizens in Philadelphia County, 1800, MS, Historical Society of Pennsylvania; Allen Johnson and Dumas Malone, eds., *Dictionary of American Biography,* 20 vols. and supplements (New York: Charles Scribner's Sons, 1928-1936); Kathryn Allamong Jacob and Bruce A. Ragsdale, eds., *Biographical Directory of the United States Congress 1774-1989* (Washington, D.C.: United States,

Government Printing Office, 1989); A Committee of the Society of the Alumni, *Biographical Catalogue of the Matriculates of the College* (Philadelphia: Printed for the Society, 1894); Society of the Alumni of the Medical Department of the University of Pennsylvania, *Catalogue of the Alumni of the Medical Department of the University of Pennsylvania. 1765-1877* (Philadelphia: Printed by Collins for the Society, 1877); University of Pennsylvania, *Alumni Master File*, microfilm, The University Archives and Record Center; Anthony N.B. Garvan, ed., *The Mutual Assurance Company Papers*, vol. 1. *The Architectural Surveys 1784-1794* (Philadelphia: The Mutual Assurance Company, 1976); Miller, *Selected Papers*, vol. 2. The single most useful source was the city directory for 1794. For the names, occupations, tax assessments, and sources used to identify specific subscribers, see my dissertation, " 'A World in Miniature': Peale's Philadelphia Museum and its Audience, 1786-1827," University of Pennsylvania, in progress.

I have adhered to Blumin's categories: "The high nonmanual category includes merchants of various kinds, brokers, professionals, and high-ranking public officials. It includes gentlemen and gentlewomen as well. The low nonmanual category includes storekeepers of all kinds, grocers, innkeepers, real estate agents, sea captains, manufacturers, clerks, accountants, and minor public officials. The high manual category includes all artisans, and the low manual category includes laborers, sailors, carters, stevedores, and a variety of other unskilled manual occupations." Stuart M. Blumin, *The Emergence of the Middle Class: Social Experience in the American City, 1760-1900* (Cambridge: Cambridge University Press, 1989), table 2.1 and p. 44, n to table 2.1.

I have made adjustments according to Blumin's observation that "school teachers, doctors and lawyers with small practices, ministers to congregations of ordinary people—also stood outside and below the urban elite on the social scale." Blumin, p.37. Because I do not have information on the size of the doctors' and lawyers' practices or the nature of the clergy's congregations, I have used an economic standard. All professionals with accumulated wealth below the 50th percentile, relative to other subscribers, were moved down the socio-economic scale to the low nonmanual category. Accumulated wealth was enumerated for 162 subscribers in the Philadelphia County Tax Assessment Ledgers, 1794-1797, for the twelve wards that comprised the city of Philadelphia, MS vols., Philadelphia City Archives.

Smith, *The "Lower Sort"*, 6.

Following is the breakdown by occupation of the Peale subscribers:

HIGH NON-MANUAL (195)
U.S. Representatives (67)
Merchants (32)
Appointed Officials, Federal and State (23)
U.S. Senators (20)
Doctors (9)
Clergymen (8)
Gentlemen (8)
Attorneys (5)
Elected Officials, City and County of Philadelphia (4)
Elected Officials, State (4)
Scriveners, Conveyancers, and Brokers (4)
Diplomats (3)
Scientists (3)
Bankers (2)
U.S. Executive Officers (2)
Dentists (1)

LOW NON-MANUAL (80)
Clerks (12)
Merchants (10)
Ironmongers (9)
Doctors (7)
Clergymen (6)
Grocers (6)
Shopkeepers (6)
Medical Students, University of Pennsylvania (5)
Attorneys (3)
Educators (3)

Sea Captains (3)
Appointed Officials, City and County of Philadelphia (2)
Inn Keepers (2)
Scriveners, Conveyancers, and Brokers (2)
Elected Officials, City and County of Philadelphia (1)
Gentlemen (1)
Manufacturers: Distillers (1)
U.S. Representatives (1)

HIGH MANUAL (38)
Leather and Cloth Workers (10)
Wood Workers (9)
Metal Workers (6)
Printers/Booksellers (4)
Apothecaries (3)
Painters and Printmakers (2)
Surveyors (2)
Agriculturalists (1)
Bakers (1)

LOW MANUAL (0)

15. Expansion into the State House, *Aurora General Advertiser*, 29 June 1802. Exhibits and fees at each location, Charles Willson Peale, "Guide to the Philadelphia Museum" (Philadelphia: Museum Press, April, 1805), in Miller, *Selected Papers*, vol. 2, pt. 2, pp. 759-66. The exhibits were later consolidated in the State House, *Poulson's American Daily Advertiser*, 5 August 1811; Catherine Fritsch, translated by A.R. Beck, "Notes of a Visit to Philadelphia, Made by a Moravian Sister in 1810," in *The Pennsylvania Magazine of History and Biography*, vol. 36, no. 3 (1912), 360; Smith, *The "Lower Sort"*, 92-125; Davidson, *Revolution and the Word*, 25.

Tickets at $1, *Pennsylvania Packet*, 21 July 1788; $2, $5, and $6 in the header to the *Subscriptions* list for 1796, 1801, and 1802 respectively; and $10, *Poulson's American Daily Advertiser*, 2 November 1819.

The "Friends of Science" are recognized in the opening inscription, dated 10 January 1794, of the *Subscriptions* volume.

16. Theater admission fees, *General Advertiser*, 14 February 1791; "A Frequenter of the Theatre", *General Advertiser*, 25 October 1794. Geraldine Duclow, Head of the Theatre Collection of the Free Library of Philadelphia, kindly shared her research on the Chestnut Street Theatre.

17. Charles Willson Peale to Rembrandt Peale, 28 October 1809, in Miller, *Collected Papers*, vol. 1, IIA/48A11 and typescript, IIA/48B5. Orosz also cites this passage in his presentation of the argument that "Peale's concept of education was essentially a didactic effort to control the lower classes," in *Curators and Culture*, 81, 83.

Timeline Credits

Page 25: Michael Angelo Peale, by Rembrandt Peale, c. 1823, Baltimore City Life Museums

Page 26 (left): General Samuel Smith, by Rembrandt Peale, 1817–18, Baltimore City Life Museums

Page 26 (right): General John Stricker, by Rembrandt Peale, 1816, Baltimore City Life Museum

Page 27 (left): Mayor Edward Johnson, by Rembrandt Peale, 1816, Baltimore City Life Museums

Page 27 (center): Lieutenant Colonel George Armistead, by Rembrandt Peale, 1817–18, Baltimore City Life Museums

Page 27 (right): Titian Ramsey Peale II, by Charles Willson Peale, 1819, Private Collection

Page 28: Sarah Miriam Peale, Self-portrait, c. 1830, Baltimore City Life Museums

Page 29 (left): Sketch of "Fast Walking Machine," by Charles Willson Peale, American Philosophical Society

Page 29 (right): Commodore Joshua Barney, by Rembrandt Peale, 1819, Baltimore City Life Museum

Page 30: Hannah Peale, by Charles Willson Peale, Museum of Fine Arts, Boston

Page 32: Charles Willson Peale, Self-portrait, The New York Historical Society

Page 33: Charles Waterton, by Charles Willson Peale, National Portrait Gallery, London

Page 34: Washington Before Yorktown, by Rembrandt Peale, The Corcoran Gallery of Art

Page 36: Philadelphia Arcade, After Charles Burton, American Philosophical Society

Page 37: Angel, by Rembrandt Peale, after Correggio, George T. Arden

Page 38: The Parthenon, New York City, artist unknown, Museum of the City of New York

Page 50: Rembrandt Peale's estimate of annual expenses, Baltimore Museum Account Book, MS.92, Maryland Historical Society

Page 51 (left): Advertisement for "The African Lion," *Baltimore American and Commercial Daily Advertiser*, September 30, 1815, Maryland Historical Society

Page 51 (right): The Roman Daughter, by Rembrandt Peale, National Museum of American Art, Smithsonian Institution, Gift of the James Smithson Society

Page 52: Advertisement with gas lighting logo, *Federal Gazette* (Baltimore), June 17, 1816, Enoch Pratt Free Library

Page 53: Advertisement for "Gas Light. The Baltimore Museum . . . " *Baltimore American and Commercial Daily Advertiser*, Maryland Historical Society

Page 54 (left): Portrait of Sena Sama, by James Warrell, Valentine Museum, Richmond, Virginia

Page 54 (right): Advertisement for "Sena Sama," *Baltimore American and Commercial Daily Advertiser*, March 18, 1818, Maryland Historical Society

Page 55 (top left): General Andrew Jackson, by Rembrandt Peale, 1819, Baltimore City Life Museums

Page 55 (bottom left): The Duke of Wellington, by Rembrandt Peale, after Sir Thomas Lawrence, Museum of Fine Arts, Boston

Page 55 (right): The Signing of the Declaration of Independence, by John Trumbull, Architect of the Capitol

Page 56 (top): Advertisement for "Court of Death, An Original Painting . . . " in *Baltimore American and Commercial Daily Advertiser*, September 2, 1820, Maryland Historical Society

Page 56 (bottom): Ariadne Asleep on the Island of Naxos, by John Vanderlyn, The Pennsylvania Academy of Fine Arts, Gift of Mrs. Sarah Harrison (The Joseph Harrison, Jr. Collection)

Page 58 (left): Night-blooming Cereus or Queen of the Night, from Robert John Thornton, *Temple of Flora* (London: 1799), Cornell University Libraries

Page 58 (right): Advertisement for "Peale's Museum," *Baltimore American and Commercial Daily Advertiser*, July 29, 1822, Maryland Historical Society

Page 59 (left): Rubens Peale's expenses for March 1823, Baltimore Museum Account Book, MS 92, Maryland Historical Society

Page 59 (right): Advertisement for Mr. Vilallave's Circus, *Baltimore American and Commercial Daily Advertiser*, November 14, 1823, Maryland Historical Society, Baltimore

Page 60 (left): Frontispiece portrait of G. Belzoni from *Narrative of the operations and recent discoveries within the pyramids, temples, tombs, and excavations in Egypt . . .* (London, 2nd ed., 1821), George Peabody Library, Johns Hopkins University

Page 60 (center): George Washington, by Rembrandt Peale, c. 1824, The Pennsylvania Academy of the Fine Arts, Gift of Mrs. Sarah Harrison (The Joseph Harrison Jr. Collection)

Page 60 (right): Marquis de Lafayette, by Rembrandt Peale, 1825, The Metropolitan Museum of Art, Rogers Fund, 1921

Page 61: Advertisement for "New Menagerie of Ten Living Animals," *Baltimore American and Commercial Daily Advertiser*, February 2, 1825, Maryland Historical Society

Page 62: Life Mask of Charles Carroll of Carrollton, by John Henri Isaac Browere, July 1826, New York State Historical Association, Cooperstown

Page 64 (left): Advertisement for "The Old Favourite Returned . . . Apollo." *Baltimore American and Commercial Daily Advertiser*, September 3, 1828, Maryland Historical Society

Page 64 (right): "The Celebrated Master Nellis, Born Without Arms," *Zoological Exhibition, N.W. Corner of Broad and Filbert Streets* (Philadelphia, 1836), The Historical Society of Pennsylvania

Page 65 (left): "Humbird and Hawkeye's Benefit . . . at the Maryland Museum," Broadside, undated, The New York Historical Society

Page 65 (right): "Miss Honeywell's Gallery of Cuttings and Needle-Work . . . " Broadside, c. 1837–48, The New York Historical Society

❀ Index